❧ The Art of Being
a Responsible Patient

PATIENTHOOD

by *MIRIAM SIEGLER*
and *HUMPHRY OSMOND*

MACMILLAN PUBLISHING CO., INC.
NEW YORK

Macmillan Publishing Co., Inc.
866 Third Avenue, New York, N.Y. 10022
Collier Macmillan Canada, Ltd.

Library of Congress Cataloging in Publication Data

Siegler, Miriam.
  Patienthood.

  Bibliography: p.
  1. Physician and patient. 2. Sick—Psychology.
I. Osmond, Humphry, joint author. II. Title.
R727.3.S53   610.69'6   79-1156
ISBN 0-02-610670-1

First Printing 1979

Printed in the United States of America

A somewhat different version of the material in
Chapter XV appeared in "The Doctor and the Dying
Role," *The Practitioner* 216 (June 1976): 690–94, and
"The Dying Role—Its Clinical Importance," *Alabama
Journal of Medical Sciences*, Vol. 13, No. 3 (1976): 313–17.
Both articles by Humphry Osmond and Miriam Siegler.

Used by permission:
  Excerpts from *Cancer Ward*, by Alexander Solzhenitsyn, translated by Nicholas Bethell and David Burg, published by The Bodley Head, London, and by Farrar, Straus & Giroux, Inc., New York, 1969.
  Excerpts from "On Being Ill," in *The Moment and Other Essays* by Virginia Woolf, published by The Hogarth Press, London, and by Harcourt Brace Jovanovich, Inc., New York, 1947. Also by permission of the Author's Literary Estate.
  Excerpts from *Return to Laughter* by Elenore Bowen copyright 1954 by Laura Bohannan. Reprinted by permission of Doubleday & Co., Inc.

*To our families,
friends, colleagues, and patients
who have,
in their different ways,
all helped us to explore,
describe, and attempt to understand
the realm of patienthood.*

MIRIAM SIEGLER

June 12, 1928–February 3, 1979

Not long after this book was begun,
Miriam Siegler suffered a series of illnesses,
the last of which was the cancer that killed her.
During those anguished years,
she weighed, tested, and tried
the ideas developed here.
Few patients
have been more responsible than she
and no one has undertaken the sick role
with more exact understanding of its duties and rights.
Her doctors, nurses, family, and friends
were awed by her courage,
resourcefulness, and determination.
Her editors and I
were astonished
that while fighting bravely for her life,
she observed and reported
the course of the battle so well.
During her final stay in the hospital,
she corrected the galley proofs
and returned them.
She was satisfied that her hard-bought knowledge
had been distilled in the pages of this book.
After this, she returned home.
On the evening of February 3, 1979,
she died in the presence of her family,
making that good end
of which it can be said
"The last act crowns the play."

H.O.

Contents

Acknowledgments

As WITH ITS PREDECESSOR, we are indebted to many people whose help made it possible for us to write this book.

Funds and other kinds of valuable support have been given by the states of New Jersey and Alabama; the Department of Psychiatry at the University of Alabama in Birmingham; Bryce Hospital, Tuscaloosa, Alabama; and the General Research Grant of the National Institutes of Health and the Robert Sterling Foundation. Our work began in 1964 with a grant from the American Schizophrenic Foundation. In 1976 its parent organization, the Huxley Institute for Biosocial Research, continued an excellent tradition by making another grant. When involuntary participant observation of the sick role by one of us imperiled the whole enterprise, a timely grant by Ms. Kathleen Ireland of Birmingham provided welcome relief and allowed this book to be completed.

We have been fortunate to have had support and encouragement from many colleagues and friends, which has maintained our morale during those doldrums with which writers are often beset. Only a few of those who have helped at one time or another can be mentioned here: Professors Patrick Linton, M.D.; John Smythies, M.D., FRCP; John Clancy, M.D., FRCP (c); Paul M. Houston, M.D.; Russell Noyes, M.D.; C. C. Pfeiffer, M.D., Ph.D.; Allie Boyd, M.D.; Harold Robb, M.D.; Hugh L'Etang, MB., BCh. (London); Erik Paterson, MBBCh; The Reverend K. Bohannan; The Reverend Carl Bretz; Morris Shumiatcher, QC D Jur (Canada); Ms. Rebecca Knox; Ms. Diane Mosbacher; and Mr. and Mrs. Glenn Ireland, II.

In a slightly different category, since they have followed our work from its earliest beginnings, are Abram Hoffer, M.D., Ph.D., FRCP (c); Frances Cheek, Ph.D.; and Robert Sommer, Ph.D. Professor T. T. Paterson (Canada) developed the concept of Aesculapian authority twenty years ago. Without it, this book could not have been written.

Robert Mullaly, Ph.D., and Cynthia Bisbee, Ph.D., have delighted us by applying the Principles of Responsible Patienthood in the Psychological Learning Center at Bryce Hospital.

We are also indebted to medical residents, medical students, and undergraduates, graduates, post graduates, and the academic staffs from several faculties at the University of Alabama (Tuscaloosa), who by careful listening and well-aimed questions have tested and tempered our ideas.

Our editors, Mr. Michael Denneny, Ms. Beth Rashbaum, and Ms. Elisabeth Scharlatt, have always been helpful and encouraging. The present plan for the book owes much to Michael Denneny's excellent advice, while Elisabeth Scharlatt has seen it through to its publication.

Mrs. Jearldine Matherson, Ms. Becky Rice, Mrs. Mary Frances Simmons, Mrs. Claudia Whisler, and Mrs. Toni Hulsey have rendered many secretarial services for which we thank them.

Introduction

DURING THE LAST FIFTY YEARS public health has greatly improved, especially in the control of infectious diseases and the reduction of infant and maternal mortality. Those of us who have benefited by these medical, scientific, and social advances have fewer opportunities to learn how to behave when we become ill. When we do get sick, it comes as a rude shock. It is no longer an expected, unavoidable part of life. Patienthood, that capacity to cope with the vicissitudes of illness, is becoming a lost art.

Because of our steadily improving health we have become far more vulnerable to the social and psychological effects of illness. We have become inept, inexperienced, and unseasoned patients; we behave like badly trained soldiers who are liable to be panicky, cowardly, and even mutinously outraged when battle joins. Too little practice has left us too ignorant to fully participate in the fight for life. Sometimes we become merely passive objects of nursing and medical skill;

even worse, we may be actively bad patients who thwart the attempts of doctors, nurses, and our families to help us survive. Bad patients, as we shall discover, are liable to become premature corpses.

We know little about our rights as patients and even less about our duties. Because of our ignorance we accept dangerous and even unnecessary treatments with unquestioning meekness while making demands upon others on matters which we could handle ourselves. We may tyrannize our families and doctors with incessant demands for treatment when exercise, proper nutrition, and attending to a prescribed regimen might greatly improve our health. This same ignorance and irresponsibility may cause us to suffer years of pain and misery from some condition which could be easily and quickly alleviated. We do not know what we have the right to expect.

The intricate and ancient "dance" between doctor and patient can be traced back to a time over sixty thousand years ago. As Doris F. Jonas points out in *Life After Death*, there is evidence in the Shanidar cave in Iraq that a prototypic doctor and patient existed. It is only in the last generation that we have forgotten the steps of the dance of life and death. Doctors themselves have become as ignorant as their patients, for there are doctors practicing today who have never been seriously ill and whose parents, siblings, spouse, and children have been equally lucky.

How can we relearn those steps so recently and inadvertently lost yet ours since time immemorial? We may need it at any moment: our lives will depend upon it. Fortunately, while the technical aspects of medicine have changed and are changing very rapidly, the rules governing the relationship between doctor and patient have altered little over the years.

After two thousand years the words of Jesus Ben Sirach in this famous passage from Ecclesiasticus are still fresh and apt:

Honour a physician with the honour due unto him for the uses which
   ye may have of him:
For the Lord hath created him
For of the most High cometh healing . . .
Let him not go from thee
For thou hast need of him
There is a time when in their hands it is good success.

However, the famous passage ends on this less reassuring
note:

He that sinneth before his Maker
Let him fall into the hands of the physician.*

We still admire doctors today, but now as then our admira-
tion is mixed with uneasiness, fear, resentment, envy, and
even more obscure feelings.

   In the past we learned the rules of patienthood in the
rough school of frequent illnesses involving family, friends,
and ourselves. Those who survived this rigorous, involuntary training not only became adept in the art of patienthood,
but were qualified to teach their children this dangerous but
unavoidable game. In the last fifty years this has all changed.
What we once learned at childbeds, sickbeds, and deathbeds
in our own homes must now be learned in hospitals. Yet the
modern hospital is not equipped for teaching such matters.
The staffs of these huge technopalaces assume that anyone
who presents him- or herself for treatment is a patient and
must know how to play the part. Television and to a lesser
extent radio, which might provide valuable social guidance,
just add to the confusion by enlarging technical knowledge
without reducing our ignorance of patienthood. For the moment, then, we must get this information from books—or not
at all.

   No one wants to be sick, and once well, as Virginia Woolf
observed shrewdly, few of us want to remember what it was

*Eccles. 38: 17–18.

like when we were ill. But we *must* learn to think about these matters; we must stop endangering ourselves with our growing ignorance.

If we are to survive illness (or even be allowed to depart in peace) with bodies and souls intact, we must maintain our self-respect. We must prepare ourselves to cope as well as possible with difficult and anguishing situations and, by so doing, become responsible patients. We must learn to play this demanding role well enough to avoid becoming unwilling guinea pigs, helpless victims, litigious malcontents, malingerers, or hypochondriacs.

The object of this book is to help you become a responsible patient. Successful patienthood helps all of us; by reasserting and reaffirming this lifesaving role, it increases the chances that we will make the very best of the medical resources available.

The Basic Elements
of Patienthood

I *The Unintended Consequences of Better Medicine*

DURING THE 1950S, a young doctor and his wife moved to a small town in middle America. He had come to work for an older practitioner whose habit it was to prescribe a "mycin" (streptomycin, Terramycin) for ailments both great and small. One day the young doctor became ill: some sort of virus, nothing to worry about. Then he began to run a high fever; it was soon so high that his "doctor's orders" to his wife (after all, he *was* the doctor) grew more and more incoherent. Finally, in a burst of irritability because he felt she did not understand how to take care of him, he hurled a candelabra at her. Luckily, some old friends chanced to visit; the wife was a nurse and quickly realized the young doctor's temperature was soaring out of control and his wife left something to be desired as a nurse.

It was late at night and no rubbing alcohol was available, but a local tavern provided ice. The doctor's wife and the two friends spent the night attempting to cool the sick doctor. It was a rough night. The doctor was a big man and several hours of work were needed to bring his temperature down even one degree; the moment they stopped their cooling operation, his temperature would shoot up again. By morning the doctor was out of danger from cooking himself to death, and he and his wife decided to summon the old G.P. and were suitably grateful when he came and prescribed a "mycin" in his usual fashion.

Now these young people were fairly typical middle-class Americans: both had parents who were alive and in good health; each had one sibling also in good health; and between them they had twenty-seven equally healthy cousins. Their childhood had been completely free of anguished childbirth scenes: the death of young siblings; all-night vigils such as the one they had just experienced; and long, drawn-out, deathbed dramas. The cries of pain, the thrashing of delirium, the groans of labor—all had been conspicuous by their absence. But these were commonplace scenes in the lives of their parents; indeed, the young wife's parents were married in 1919, the year of the Spanish influenza, a pandemic which took the lives of twenty-one million people in 120 days. What was it like to be married during the year in which some scientists believed the world's population might be wiped out by the worst medical disaster of all time? One would think this to be a never-to-be-forgotten tale the horror of which would be passed along from generation to generation. But memories of such events seem curiously deficient, for the young wife had never heard about the epidemic, nor, it seems, about any aspect of illness.

The young doctor and his wife were not Christian Scientists, nor did they subscribe to any doctrine of mind over matter. They simply believed what no one fifty years earlier would have dared to believe: they were entitled, as a birthright, to perfect health for themselves and all members of their family. The progress of medicine, of which they were the fortunate but ignorant beneficiaries, had left them totally unprepared for the occurrence of illness.

This couple had twenty-seven cousins; their two children had only five. Contraception makes it possible to have a small number of children, and the knowledge that each of these planned-for children will survive makes it desirable to have only the number of children one wants to raise. Increased life expectancy has further altered family life: it is possible for some children, like those of the doctor and his wife, to go through childhood with four living grandparents.

Most of the world's population does not share this good fortune, most Americans do not; in fact, most middle-class Americans are not as entirely free of the experience of illness as this particular young couple. What these young people take for granted has an influence far beyond its actual occurrence; it has colored the way illness and death are perceived and has changed our attempts to cope with them. It has necessitated what would have been absurd fifty years ago: the need for this book.

Of all the changes which have taken place since the beginning of this century, perhaps none has affected family life as much as the decrease in the mortality of children. Today, in Europe and North America, one child in forty dies in his first year; in Africa, the figure is still one in seven. Anthropologist Laura Bohannan, in *Return to Laughter*, a fictionalized account of her field work in Nigeria in the early 1950s, reports an even higher death rate. When she tried to express sympathy to a mother who had just lost a child, the child's mother said, "It is nothing. She just died. Children often die. It is their nature." The author writes, "I had nothing to say. Nothing in my own life or in my own land had prepared me for this. Poorgbilin's senior wife sat down beside her and took a handful of beans to shell. 'I have borne ten children. . . . Of the ten, seven died; but three are living. Now I have grandchildren. You too will someday hold a grandchild on your lap. Then you will know it was not in vain.' "

In his later years, Samuel Johnson befriended a wealthy and privileged young couple, Henry and Hester Thrale. He was a frequent visitor, almost a family member, at Streatham, the Thrales' estate near London. The life at Streatham was elegant, the countryside beautiful, the dinner conversation brilliant. But all this was worthless in the family life of the Thrales, for they lost seven of their eleven children. Hester Thrale was for many years either pregnant, in mourning, or both, and her husband took to spending more and more time with his mistresses in London, who were no doubt better company than his unhappy wife. For Hester, nothing could make up for the loss of seven children—not even having Samuel Johnson as a houseguest.

Suppose, then, that one can control the size of one's family with contraception, that one survives childbirth, and that one lives with the expectation that all of one's planned-for children will survive into adulthood: what happens when one of these children develops a fatal disease? Far from believing it is the nature of children to die, these parents believe they have been visited by a totally unexpected calamity. In *Eric*, Doris Lund, writing of the fatal illness of her son, said, "A tremendous flash split the world. The bolt entered the top of my skull, as I got the message. Eric has leukemia. It was something happening right this minute in his bones. We'd been struck. It was ours." Starting with John Gunther's *Death Be Not Proud*, a new genre of literature has appeared: a grieving parent writes the story of the illness of a beloved child who died in spite of having available every resource of modern medicine. These books—*Death Be Not Proud, Eric, Ellen: A Short Life Long Remembered* by Rose Levit, *The Story of Josh* by Marcia Friedman—are beautifully written memorials, ennobling accounts of love and courage in the face of death. But they would not have made any sense to Hester Thrale, or even to our own grandmothers. In order to write such a book, one must first assume that children grow up healthy, and if they do become ill, medical science will cure them.

At a time when many children died, those who survived learned valuable lessons in patienthood: when to report injuries or symptoms to their parents, how to read the doctor's face, when to avoid other children sick with contagious diseases, which illnesses were considered serious. They watched their siblings die, and they themselves survived illnesses which, though trivial today, might easily have carried them off. One man, writing of his boyhood in the 1920s, said:

I still remember the large place sickness had in our village in the south of England. A mere sore throat might herald the terrifying diphtheria and old Dr. Hall was always being sent for. He was not a talkative man, but solid and very reassuring. He would grunt and pound your chest, grunt again and prod your belly. My knee got infected one day and Dr. Hall was sent for. I remember his looking at it and pulling first his handlebar moustache and then his ear lobe, as was his custom. Then he blew his nose loudly. I discovered later that this meant he was puzzled and had made a decision. He soon came back with another doctor who agreed that they must operate, for there were no antibiotics then. Operations were usually done at home, hospitals being for the indigent in those days. Soon my room became the center of activity and there were all kinds of mysterious preparations. Furniture was moved, sheets hung on the walls, a kitchen table brought near the window. I didn't know what was happening, but when my father said, "There's nothing to worry about, old fellow," and gripped my hand tightly, my excitement became tinged with fear.

It was a small operation, but our household was quite disorganized by it. We had a nurse for a short time and then my aunts nursed me. My little sister could only peek in at me. It was rather grand at first but I soon became lonely. Dr. Hall was very concerned that the wound stayed clean so its edges were rubbed with a caustic "blue stone" which hurt and made me howl. I spent many weeks in bed and healed slowly. I've always suspected the agonizing blue stone. I have never understood why I was abed so long with such a trivial ailment, but it seems to have been the custom. When I tried to walk after more than six weeks in bed, I couldn't even stand. It was another month or so before I was running around with my sister. This showed how ill I had been.

For nearly three months Dr. Hall's word was law in our house. I recall how cheerful we all felt when he said that all was well and how gloomy we became when he seemed gloomy. Every time he came to look at my operation I would scrutinize his impassive face. I became skilled at reading it, for I was afraid of the horrible blue stone. When at last I was running around, if I fell down and grazed my leg I would be hurried in and anointed with seaweed smelling, stingy iodine, for Dr. Hall had saved my leg once and might not be able to do it a second time. I held him in reverence, since in spite of the thrilling possibilities of being a peg-leg, I didn't really want to be like Long John Silver.

When I was well again, no one in our family needed to be lectured about doctors or had any doubt about their skill, judgement and devotion. What is more, everyone in our village knew that if it hadn't been for Dr. Hall, I might have lost a leg or worse.

More recently, Stephan Lesher, a thirty-eight-year-old Washington correspondent, suffered a heart attack and entered the hospital for the first time in his life. In an article entitled "After a Heart Attack," which appeared in the *New York Times Magazine,* he said: "I was no more prepared emotionally for a heart attack than the citizenry was prepared to believe their G.I.'s could slaughter at My Lai." This child of the post-antibiotic era, reared well out of sight of the shadow of death, made a poor patient. He refused to take some of the medications prescribed for him and devoted himself instead to becoming a pseudoexpert on heart disease with his wardmates. He managed to survive his own amateur status as a patient and willy-nilly made some sort of adjustment to his new condition. He even wrote a book about his experience, *A Coronary Event,* co-authored by his doctor, Michael Halberstam.

When someone is admitted to a hospital, a history is taken

in which the patient is asked about his previous illnesses and hospitalizations. When there is no previous history, this is naturally regarded with some pride by the patient and is often seen as a good thing by the staff member taking the history. Perhaps the time has come to look at these questions from a wholly different point of view. Anyone who answers no to the question "Have you ever been seriously ill?" is telling the doctor that he has had no previous experience in the sick role and is therefore in danger of not knowing how to conduct himself as a patient. If a patient comes from a notably healthy family and has no recollection of parents, siblings, or grandparents being ill, the situation is even more perilous. The better preventive medicine works in childhood, the worse adults are prepared to handle illness. This is an unprecedented state of affairs, an unintended consequence of better public health and clinical medicine.

The man with the infected knee had months in which to learn the rules of patienthood, and since he was about six at the time of the illness that knowledge remained with him for more than half a century. The lengthy and intimate relationship which then prevailed between doctor and patient was also the school in which the patient learned, in slow motion as it were, the give-and-take of "doctor's orders" and patient compliance. The whole process was so slow that there was plenty of time for both parties to correct their misconceptions about each other's intentions and behavior. Now, lengths of both illnesses and hospitalizations have been greatly shortened.

Recently, a very intelligent, well-educated, and sophisticated man developed cerebral malaria shortly after a visit to Africa. He was admitted to a London hospital one Sunday in a coma. He remembers little about that week until Wednesday. By Friday he was talking about leaving the hospital, and on Monday morning he was discharged.

What did he think of the medical profession who had hustled him out so fast? When asked about his doctor, he said,

"Very interesting fellow, but I didn't see too much of him." However, he did feel he had been treated well. That was all. He certainly did not grasp that he had been saved, by rapid and skillful diagnosis combined with well-aimed and effective treatment, from an affliction which was nearly always fatal in the not too distant past. If it was treated successfully, recovery from cerebral malaria was slow and required months of patient skill. But this man's convalescence was not marked by any special diets—no champagne jellies, no stout or ale, not even a glass of port in the evenings. Just a few rather insignificant-looking white pills to take for a couple of weeks. In a word, he did not feel as if he had been under a doctor's care. He had merely been delivered from probable death or, at the least, a very long and unpleasant illness by the skills, techniques, and drugs used today by the medical profession. He did not feel personally indebted to a particular doctor because he had not been and did not require to be treated personally.

Expectations from improved diagnostic capabilities have gone up along with those of prevention and treatment. No one really expects to die of an undiagnosed illness anymore. Yet the rarity of once-familiar illnesses has made their diagnosis more difficult. For example, the successful treatment of anthrax depends on prompt diagnosis, yet few American doctors have ever seen a case. Five Americans died of anthrax in 1964; ironically, these five might have lived if the disease were more prevalent. Gout and pellagra are two other diseases which are more often misdiagnosed now than in the past. Patients who expect a continuous improvement in diagnostic acumen may be especially angry if the diagnosis of some once-common disease is missed.

Our expectations have risen to dizzying heights in the areas of infant survival, longevity, rapid and effective treatment, and accurate diagnosis. We also expect that when someone contracts a fatal illness, he will die fairly quickly and comfortably. It therefore comes as a shock to many families that the fatal illness of one of their members may last for several years, cause great pain and suffering for the patient, absorb all of the family's financial resources, and totally disorganize their lives. The gains that have been made in medical treatment now enable fatally ill people to survive for much longer than was formerly possible, but not necessarily with any marked benefit to themselves or their families. Doctors, patients, and families alike are now caught in a trap where technological advances have far outstripped the social machinery for dealing with immanent death. No one knows who has the right to blow the whistle; all parties want to behave ethically, yet the result may be, as Enid Nemy put it in an article in the *New York Times,* "a very real experience in hell."

Nothing fails like success. The expectations have risen, the performance has improved, but the gap between them has widened. The result: a malpractice crisis. Patients have taken to suing their doctors in greater and greater numbers, for larger and larger amounts. Both doctors and patients are baffled and hurt by their deteriorating relationship, and, like an unhappy couple, they have carried their quarrel to the courts. But the law is a blunt instrument, and while it can recompense an injured party, it cannot improve the damaged doctor-patient relationship which, unlike a marriage, must go on.

How does this look from the doctor's point of view? An anonymous gynecologist, in his memoir *Confessions of a Gynecologist,* wonders why a lifetime of greatly improved medical care for his mothers and babies has resulted in worsening relations and increasing lawsuits. The fact is, medicine has altered greatly but doctors have not. They have created a revolution in expectations, but have they noticed it? The life of the practitioner has remained essentially the same as ever: he sees a limited number of sick people, and he does his best for them. His predicament is much like that of the modern housewife: washers, dryers, freezers, microwave ovens, and other advances in technology have made many luxuries possible, but the increase in expectations has wiped out the hoped-for increase in status and prestige. Meanwhile, the role has not altered much at all. Doctors, like homemakers, are craftspeople. They are inherently conservative about their work, for in any craft, innovations are as likely to be for the worse as for the better.

Although clinical medicine has changed greatly in the last fifty years, it has *not* become an applied science—anymore than motherhood has become applied clinical psychology. Abraham Flexner, in his famous report to the Carnegie Foundation in 1910, was wrong to believe that science medicine was about to cause clinical medicine, like the Marxist state, to wither away. Clinical medicine is not reducible to science or public health medicine because it is a practical craft concerned, always, with the ill person and his or her family. Because of scientific advances and social changes, some illnesses have disappeared, but each single human being still lives in a fragile body which can, and ultimately will, suffer illness, injury, and death.

Throughout the centuries the threat of death was the doctor's best friend. Death, not Blue Cross, was the third party in the doctor-patient transaction. Death remains, but screened by our illusions of perfect health; it is only because we so seldom meet death face to face that we dare to quarrel with or belittle our doctors. The most favorable accounts of doctors are found in those books in which parents write of the death of their children. When things get really bad, the doctor-patient relationship often improves. Doctors and patients have been held together for centuries, millennia even, by the inescapable presence of death. Now that we have the good fortune to be a little more distant from death, more hopeful about the outcome of illness, we can no longer rely on this extremely effective control on our relationship.

Another casualty of improved medicine is the decline in the prestige of nurses. The early Nightingale nurses knew that doctors were not gods—their patients died all too frequently. Good nursing often made the difference between life and death. It was because of the incompetence of nurses that Florence Nightingale began her great work in the Crimea. Doctors did not take good nursing for granted; no one who had ever tried to practice hospital medicine without it could possibly be so foolish. As for nursing at home, there are many accounts of the efforts of frightened amateurs to deal with serious illness and death. While no one wishes for prolonged or unnecessary hospitalization, those who romanticize treatment in the home seldom remember that it was tried for centuries.

The expectation of a long and healthy life is one of the great social revolutions of our time. We have not even begun to understand its implications for the practice of medicine. While older doctors, like our anonymous gynecologist, are puzzled and hurt by their patients' lack of appreciation, some of the younger doctors are being affected quite differently. For the first time we are seeing frivolous doctors, doctors for whom medicine is just a game. We have always had greedy doctors, stupid doctors, pompous doctors, and mad-scientist doctors, but we have never before had doctors who do not believe in the reality of their own decay and demise anymore than they believe that the sufferings of their patients are real. They come close to being closet Christian Scientists—until they get sick. Then their expectations of what medicine can do for them are as unrealistic as those of their worst patients.

Because doctors also get sick, we trust they will be as interested as we are in refurbishing the doctor-patient relationship. As Samuel Johnson said, "A man, sir, should keep his friendships in repair." The doctor-patient relationship is just as indispensable and it, too, needs to be kept in constant repair. It is very battered at the moment, due, ironically, to the enormous progress in preventive and clinical medicine. It needs a general overhaul and a few new parts, including a new vocabulary for discussing matters which had been obvious merely by the dire circumstances under which doctor and patient met. It is our purpose here to undertake the much-needed repair job and to update the faltering social machinery to bring it into line with modern medicine and modern needs.

II *The Sick Role and Aesculapian Authority*

A FORTY-YEAR-OLD NEANDERTHAL MAN named Shanidar I by his discoverers can teach us a great deal about how his people treated their sick, impaired, and dead. Dr. Ralph Solecki and his team, exploring the Shanidar cave in Iraq in the 1950s, found a number of Neanderthal skeletons. Doris Jonas reported what Dr. Solecki learned about Shanidar I:

The most interesting aspect of this particular skeleton was that although his right shoulder blade, collar-bone and upper arm were undeveloped from birth, and the useless right arm appeared to have been amputated early in life, it was nevertheless about forty years old at the time of death, a very old man for a Neanderthal. Moreover he must have been blind in his left eye, since he had extensive bone scar tissue on the left side of his face. And, as if this were not enough, the top right side of his head had received some damage that had healed before the time of his death. In short, Shanidar I was at a distinct disadvantage in an environment where men, even in the best condition, lived hard lives. Yet he had been allowed to live. That he had made himself useful around the hearth (two hearths were found close to him) is evidenced by his unusually worn front teeth—which he had apparently used for grasping in lieu of his right arm. But since he could hardly have foraged or fended for himself, one must assume that he was accepted and supported by his people to the day he died. The stone heap found over his skeleton and the near-by mammal food remains show that even in death he was an object of some regard.

What Shanidar I tells us is that sixty thousand years ago there was a special role for an ill or injured person. He was cared for, even though he could not pull his full weight in his community. He was evidently not held to blame for being ill and impaired. The amputation shows that he received—and accepted—surgical attention and probably medical aftercare. We can also assume that he tried to recover as quickly as possible from his various wounds and that he cooperated with those trying to help him. The behavior manifested by Shanidar I and those close to him is so ancient, so universal among human cultures, and so utterly taken for granted that it had no name until 1951 when sociologist Talcott Parsons, in *The Social System*, described it and called it the "sick role."

In all cultures people fall ill and they, their families, and their friends must cope with this misfortune. In every culture, illness is regarded as a "bad" thing. Nowhere in the world, in any language, do people say: "Oh, how happy I am to feel so ill." Anthropologist W. Lloyd Warner, studying an Australian aborigine people in the 1920s, found that although both the causes and treatments for disease were very different from those of his own culture, the evaluation of illness as a bad thing was very much the same. In *A Black Civilization* he says:

A prerequisite for social conditioning and adjustment is a normal organism, normal not only in the biological fact but also in the values of the group. The normal human being not only among the savage Murngin but in any society, according to the evaluations of the group, is the "well" person. Sickness is felt by civilized man to be expectable but not normal, largely because sickness interferes with his ordinary participation in his culture. Both the savage and the civilized man consider sickness out of the ordinary, even though all organisms experience it, not only because of the lack of physical well-being but because the individual's daily social life is changed.

A striking example of the cross-cultural nature of the sick role appears in the story of Ishi, the last Stone-Age Indian in America, as told in Theodora Kroeber's *Ishi in Two Worlds*. In 1911, Ishi stumbled into the twentieth century in California and was "adopted" by two anthropologists from the university. His tribe had nearly been exterminated by the white settlers a century before; the remaining band had died out except for Ishi, who had been left utterly alone for the last three years. No one spoke his language. A home was made for him at the museum in San Francisco. Since there was no fund for the support of Stone-Age Indians, the anthropologists ingeniously put him on the payroll as a janitorial assistant. This pleased Ishi, for he had observed that everyone in the white-man's world had a regular job for which he was paid a regular wage. In addition to his paid job, Ishi gave demonstrations of his many crafts and skills for the museum visitors.

Next door to the museum was the university's medical school and hospital. Ishi soon became friends with a surgeon, Dr. Pope. Ishi taught his new friend how to make and use bows and arrows, in return for which Dr. Pope allowed Ishi to watch his operations. Being a hunter, Ishi was very knowledgeable about anatomy, and as a craftsman, he was most impressed with Dr. Pope's array of delicate instruments. Ishi watched "Popey" remove a diseased kidney and then followed the patient day by day until he recovered. After this, Ishi acknowledged that Popey was a born *kuwi*, one who could become a great Yana doctor, if only he would fast and observe the strict taboos which would allow him to receive the necessary vision.

Ishi "made rounds" at the hospital, paying brief but

frequent visits to the wards. He would stop at each bed with his hands folded in front of him. If the patient was asleep or looked too ill to notice him, he would look into the face concernedly, in silence; if the patient was awake, he would smile, say some words in Yahi, and wave as he left the room.

Some aspects of modern medicine were strange or repellent to Ishi. The morgue, into which he wandered by mistake, terrified him; he felt that dead bodies were dangerous and contaminating. Anaesthesia worried him: could the surgeon who had caused the soul to leave the body really be powerful enough to restore it so that the patient would not die of soul-loss? Interestingly enough, he thought that tonsillectomy was an unnecessary operation, a view which many have come to share. What was perfectly familiar to him was that people became ill; that when ill, they were not able to carry out their usual responsibilities and were not blamed for this; that they tried to get well; and that they accepted medical help, even when painful and frightening.

In 1914, Ishi himself developed tuberculosis and became a patient at the hospital. He occupied the sick role with great dignity, and when it became clear that nothing further could be done for him medically, he left the sick role for the dying role. He returned "home" to the museum to die among his friends. All the centuries that had intervened between the formation of Ishi's culture and that of twentieth-century California had not changed these essential elements of illness and death.

Everywhere in the world, people value the sick role and seek good medical care. When Laura Bohannan went to Nigeria to do her field work, she was warned by other anthropologists that she would be expected to provide medicine for the people whom she wished to study. She soon found that her amateur services were in such demand that she had to schedule a morning sick call so that she would have time left for the field work for which she had come to Africa. She hated being pressed into the role of healer; she was deeply disturbed by the suffering she saw, much of which she felt was unnecessary; she found the medical work itself revolting; and most of all, she hated her own incompetence and inadequacy at treating their ills with a handful of pills and simple remedies. At first she felt she had to do it to repay them for being her informants. But then, she says, "I comprehended for the first time that it is morally impossible to refuse help which it is in one's power to give." Thus she stumbled upon the other half of the doctor-patient equation: the sick person has rights and duties that imply the presence of another person, the doctor or healer, for whom the patient's duties are his rights; the patient's rights, his duties.

The cultural need for healers is exemplified in the story of Cabeza de Vaca, a Spanish explorer whose party was shipwrecked off the coast of Texas in 1528. The local Indians, who had never seen white men, decided that these unexpected visitors should become their physicians. The Spaniards protested that they had no knowledge of medicine. However, the Indians managed to persuade the Spaniards to change their minds by withholding food until they agreed. Their future patients then instructed them in the local medical arts, and they soon became proficient at it and were held in high esteem. Dr. Jesse Thompson, in an article which appeared in the *New England Journal of Medicine*, quotes Cabeza de Vaca: "They brought us their sick, which, we having blessed, they declared were sound; he who was healed, believed we could cure him." In 1535, de Vaca crowned his career as a healer by removing an arrowhead from the chest of an Indian—the first recorded surgical procedure in the American Southwest. Isolated communities today that are in need of a physician might give some thought to the unorthodox but effective methods of this enterprising tribe.

If the patients of the world share the sick role, what then do its healers have in common? They do not necessarily have a higher economic status than their fellow citizens, although the Puyallup shamans of Puget Sound live in bigger houses than their neighbors. They do not all work full time as healers; the Yemenite moris also practice a trade, such as silversmithing, and surgeons of old were barbers. They differ in the manner in which they are paid: a Yoruba medicine man or an Apache shaman expects to be paid before the treatment begins; some Yemenite moris do not ask a fee at all, while others have been known to demand a fee each month in order to get rid of a spell. In the Yoruba treatment centers, the high rate of relapse is attributed to the failure of families to pay for sufficient treatment, especially for the discharge ceremonies. As Raymond Prince observes in "Indigenous Yoruba Psychiatry," the Yoruba healers believe they can cure anything—"If there is money!" Apparently the method and amount of payment is not a universal feature of the doctor-patient relationship.

All over the world healers explain their failures by saying that the patient was not brought in soon enough, that their instructions were not carried out, or that the illness is incurable. In "The Role of Native Doctors in Aboriginal Australia," Catherine Berndt writes that in Australia a West Arnhem Land margidbu will say, "He will die. You have called me too late."

Quackery, too, is a worldwide concern, for everywhere, especially at fairs, markets, and supermarkets, the unscrupulous can make money by peddling nostrums to the gullible. The St. Lawrence Island Eskimos express this by distinguishing four grades of shaman: "really shaman," "sort of shaman," "partly shaman," and "foolish shaman"—the latter meaning quack. Because sick people are likely to be frightened and miserable, they are extremely vulnerable to anyone claiming to heal them, so people everywhere are concerned with the moral qualities of their healers. In the West this is expressed in the Hippocratic oath, but in every culture, healers must be upstanding and trustworthy members of their particular community or, as in the case of Laura Bohannan and Cabeza de Vaca, valued foreigners. In order to follow the healer's advice, which usually involves expense, disgust, pain, and danger, the patient must feel that the healer is trustworthy. But trustworthy to do what? There can be no guarantee of success in any healing system. In fact, the eventual outcome of all healing efforts is the same: the patient dies, and so does the doctor! One must trust the healer *to act in one's best interest*. The patient's intent to get well must be matched by the healer's intent to do his best for that particular patient.

It follows from this aspect of doctor-patient complementarity that the relationship is endangered either when the doctor suspects that the patient has some other intent than to get well or when the patient suspects that the doctor has some other intent than to get him well. The first is called malingering and is very much frowned upon. Children are taught at a very early age that it is wrong to pretend to be sick. A two-year-old girl of our acquaintance came out of her room one morning looking quite unwell and said, "Sick!" This was the first time she had used the word, associating it correctly with not feeling well. This drew all sorts of kind, comforting, and admiring behavior from her family. However, the next day, evidently recovered, she said, "Sick!" in order to lay claim to a can of soda which her father was drinking. This did not produce the same result; she got neither the solicitous behavior nor the soda.

In addition to being wrong, malingering is dangerous to the malingerer. Like the boy who cried "Wolf!", the child who always claims to be sick will not be believed when he really is sick. The likelihood of children malingering has increased, for many illnesses and medical treatments are not nearly as horrible as they once were. It may seem like fun to play at being sick, and a toy doctor's bag today often contains candy pills not very different from the candy-coated medicine the child might get if he were really sick. The sick role must be learned through play for those children who grow up in households where there is no real sickness to learn from. Those children who are most gifted at role playing—the ones who are always begging to have bandages put on them—will be most tempted to malinger. They must be carefully taught to distinguish the rehearsal from the real performance.

If doctors demand, as a bare minimum, that their patients be really sick and not malingering, what do patients demand of their doctors that is comparable? The doctor must have moral authority: a legitimized status in the community, a level of moral behavior acceptable to that particular community, and the intent to do what is best for the patient. The doctor must have sapiential authority: he must have or appear to have whatever kind and degree of medical knowledge considered necessary in his community. He also must have charismatic authority: he must appear to be in touch with forces greater than mere reason and technical skill, a qualification more obvious in a community permeated with religious belief. We all want to see the white coat, the stethoscope, or some other symbol of a person who is above mere mortal concerns. These three kinds of authority constitute what Professor T. T. Patterson has called Aesculapian authority. It is unique to medicine, and it can and does overrule every other kind of authority where a sick person is concerned.

Americans, who are constantly fussing and fuming about their rights, are meek as lambs when Aesculapian authority is displayed. When former President Nixon was in Long Beach Memorial Hospital his doctor went on national television and said, "Today Mr. Nixon has been given bathroom privileges." And we all nodded. But suppose then-President Ford had announced on national television, "Today I have given Mr. Nixon bathroom privileges." We would have thought that he had lost his mind! We all know that Mr. Ford, although holding the highest position of structural authority in the land, had no right to give or withhold Mr. Nixon's bathroom privileges. Pardon, yes; bathroom privileges, no. But Mr. Nixon's doctor, however obscure, had such a right because Mr. Nixon was in the sick role in relation to him, and he had Aesculapian authority in relation to Mr. Nixon. It is understood that doctors can tell presidents, ex-presidents, kings, generals, judges, popes, and prime ministers whether or not they may use the bathroom; when they may get out of bed; what medicines they must take; and what procedures they must submit to—surely a very powerful authority.

When the late Howard Hughes was in London, a small news item in the *Daily Express*, which also appeared in the August 31, 1973 edition of the *New York Times*, reported that he had entreated his doctors to operate in his hotel room to repair a broken bone in his hip. The doctors, however, told Mr. Hughes that such an operation had to be performed in a hospital. Even a very rich, eccentric, and willful man does not wish to anger his physicians, so Mr. Hughes went along to the hospital as directed. A man who *could* have overridden his doctors' authority would have thereby cut himself off from getting the best medical treatment.*

When the future King Edward VII fell ill with some intestinal disorder in 1902, just before his coronation, he pitted his structural, charismatic, and personal authority directly against the Aesculapian authority of his physicians—and lost. Dr. John Treves, Lord Lister, and Sir Thomas Smith were of the opinion that he had appendicitis; Treves, who was an authority on this particular ailment, advised immediate surgery. Edward had been waiting an inordinately long time for his coronation because of Queen Victoria's longevity. A very obstinate man, Edward was determined to be crowned on the day planned. "In that case, sir," Treves is re-

---

* In his later years, Hughes *did* succeed in overriding the Aesculapian authority of his doctors, very much to his own detriment. According to attorneys retained by the Hughes's estate, he spent his last days in a condition worse than that of the most regressed mental patients. (Donald L. Bartlett and James B. Steele, "His lawyers call Hughes a psychotic," *The Philadelphia Inquirer*, June 13, 1978.)

ported to have said, "you will go to the Abbey as a corpse."
Treves operated successfully on what was to have been coronation day. He and the king remained on the best of terms
throughout the king's life.

Even animals are not immune from Aesculapian authority.
A woman took her large and ferocious Doberman to a vet-
erinarian for treatment. The dog growled viciously and
would not let the vet approach. The vet then hit the dog with
a strap, tied it, and hit it several more times. He then treated
the dog and saved its life. A woman in the outer office, hearing the dog's cries of pain, brought the vet to court on
charges of cruelty to animals. The vet defended himself on
the grounds that he had to establish his authority with the
dog in order to treat it. After the injection, he said, he took
the dog out for a walk on a leash and the dog was friendly
toward him. The judge found him not guilty. It is worth noting that the dog's owner did not stop the vet from beating
the dog, nor did she complain. In this she resembled Queen
Alexandra, who was present when Dr. Treves exerted his authority over her husband King Edward. Treves in fact was
tougher than the vet, for the punishment he threatened was
death, not merely a few lashes.

What would be the consequences if there were no Aesculapian authority and no sick role? Mr. Nixon, Mr. Hughes,
King Edward, and the Doberman—as well as thousands of
ordinary people and animals whose stories have not been
recorded—would not have agreed to treatment and might
have died. It's difficult to follow medical advice: we don't
want to take time off from work or play; we don't want to
leave our children; we fear pain; we fear the treatment
(usually with good reason); we fear having to depend on
others; we dislike the loss of control over our own bodies; we
resent the invasion of privacy; we worry about the expense.
Yet unless we agree we cannot be treated, and so Aesculapian authority must be powerful enough to override
our objections.

If there were no Aesculapian authority, there would be no special class of healers; we would all treat ourselves and each other. In fact, most of the time we do just that since the bulk of all illness is not brought to doctors, but ignored, endured, or treated with home remedies. It is when the illness refuses to go away, when it gets suddenly worse, when the pain is unbearable, or when we fear that the outcome will be fatal that we seek out a member of that special class whom we have designated as healers. In addition to his authority in getting us to agree to treatment, the healer has the advantage of accumulated experience. All that his culture knows, his teachers can convey, and he can absorb, is passed on to him by the previous generation of healers.

People who are ill are cared for by others, usually by their families. But what happens when a culture loses the sick role or does not appear to have it? In *The Gentle Tasaday,* John Nance tells about the discovery in 1971 of the Tasaday, a small group of Stone-Age people who live in the rain forests of the Philippines. Unlike the Neanderthals and Ishi's tribe, "They admitted to no medical charms, practices, or ceremonies, and said a sick person was left to die alone. There was a hazy reference to a sickness, which, after exchanges among the translators, came out as a dreaded epidemic disease that frightened the Tasaday and had caused their ancestors to flee from someplace and, perhaps, into the forest."

The observing team included a doctor who found the health of the tribe to be excellent. One day, however, the team discovered that Lobo, a boy of about ten, had developed a fever, diarrhea, and vomiting. His mother said he was going to die, and the Tasaday were prepared to follow their usual practice of putting him out of the cave to die alone. Members of the team told them that Lobo's illness was not serious, and the Tasaday agreed to allow the team to care for Lobo—but not in the tribe's cave. They were very grateful when Lobo recovered.

When Charles Lindbergh visited the Tasaday he asked

them what was the best thing their contact with the outside world had brought them. What did they like best—knives, cloth, medicine, bow and arrow? One said, "Dokoto [doctor] is best." "You mean medicine is best?" "Yes, Dokoto and medicine."

We have no way of knowing whether the Tasaday had ever had a sick role before, but we do know that in severe epidemics the sick role may temporarily disappear. If the sick role is to be conferred it is necessary for there to be a ratio of well people to sick people. If too great a proportion of a population is sick, the fear of contagion overrides the usual medical practices and flight, rather than care, is the order of the day. It did not take the Tasaday very long to learn to appreciate the undeniable benefits of the sick role and medical practice.

People tend to blame themselves for illness, their own or those of people they love. They wonder if they have done something wrong or if they have angered the gods in some way. When he learned of his son's malignant brain tumor, Leib Friedman said, "What have we done wrong?" The reaction is a natural one, even though no one has suggested that brain tumors are caused by faulty parenting or anything else over which we have control. His wife Marcia, in her book *The Story of Josh*, quickly put an end to this line of reasoning, "I felt that if we didn't at this moment expunge all sense of personal guilt, we would be unable to function in Josh's best interests." Yet later, when a friend began to hint at some cause or purpose to Josh's illness, she succumbed to self-blame. After Josh's death, however, she listened to the tapes he had made during the last months of his illness and was greatly comforted to find that her son, far from blaming his parents, expressed his gratitude for the confidence and strength they had given him. The sick role therefore also makes it possible to avoid useless self-blame which can interfere with treatment—maybe its most important function.

Some illnesses have symptoms which make normal social

functioning difficult or impossible. In Irvin Ashkenazy's story, "Judy Has Myasthenia Gravis," we learn of a woman, with undiagnosed myasthenia gravis, who had been growing steadily weaker and more depressed. Her husband, hoping to cheer her up, took her out to dinner. During the meal he said, "You're not mad at me, are you? You look so . . . so angry." His wife was astonished at this and said that of course she was not angry. But a glance at her pocket mirror showed that her facial muscles were drooping into an unconscious scowl. This increased her feeling that she was becoming a burden to her husband. These misunderstandings were cleared up only when she was finally diagnosed as having myasthenia and safely installed in the sick role. Without the sick role there would not have been any explanation for her scowling that would not have been damaging to their relationship. Could it mean that she did not like the meal? That she did not enjoy his company? That their marriage was in jeopardy? The sick role makes it possible to say, "I see that you are getting tired—your facial muscles are drooping. Would you rather go home now?"

These, then, are the basic elements of patienthood: a *reciprocal relationship* between a sick person and a healer in which the healer does his best for the patient and the patient tries his best to get well. The benefits of this social invention are that the patient may have a better chance to survive, that his suffering may be diminished, and that his social relations are not disrupted by self-blame or the blame of others. *Aesculapian authority* provides the patient with someone he can trust and from whom he can accept treatment. It also helps to provide a body of medical knowledge which accumulates and is passed along from one generation of healers to the next.

This relationship can go askew in a number of ways. The patient can malinger (although this seems to be rare). He can show too much medical piety or too little. He can use his illness to tyrannize others. He can fail to cooperate with the treatment or he can expect unreasonable results from the treatment. He can be outraged at the very idea of being ill and so deny himself the sick role.

The doctor, too, can misuse his Aesculapian authority. He can use it for some purpose other than conferring the sick role and treating patients. This is what some psychiatrists have done: they have undertaken an ever-increasing number of activities which take them further and further away from actually treating patients. They are now using their Aesculapian authority to advocate political programs, change community relations, denounce families, advise about the mental health of statesmen, apply psychoanalytic ideas to historical figures, etc. No one has asked them to undertake these activities, at which they are amateurs. Thickly insulated with Aesculapian authority, which they do not know they have and therefore have no reason to give up, they press ahead with more and more grandiose projects while the care and treatment of their patients is neglected.

In general medicine the error has been in the other direction: the patient is still there, but due to the vast burgeoning of technical and scientific medicine, he has been reduced to a mere object upon whom these technical wonders will be performed. The doctor has in effect hung a sign upon his neck: "Quiet. Genius at work." And the patient has not yet learned to say, "You must answer my questions because you are here only for me."

Aesculapian authority exists only for the benefit of sick people. It is chemically bound, as it were, to the particular, individual, unique, irreducible patient. When it comes unbound it becomes a very powerful and dangerous force. That is why it is so important that we learn to "see" it and so be able to judge whether or not it is being used legitimately.

III *Acquiring the Sick Role*

THE LINE THAT SEPARATES the well role from the sick role is invisible; yet we must learn to see it because life on the other side of that line is utterly different and played by different rules. We must learn to recognize when someone who needs the sick role fails to get it or refuses it, or when someone who doesn't need or want the sick role is given it. We must be able to follow the progress of the person who has left the sick role for the dying role, the impaired role, the guinea pig role, the "psych" role—or for no role at all, a roleless limbo. Only when the sick role stands out in sharp relief will we be able to make conscious choices about it instead of being swept along by events over which we have no control.

When the sick role is both needed and accepted the transaction can occur with astonishing speed. In "Sir James Paget," Ralph Major tells the story of a Yorkshireman who consulted Sir James Paget. The Yorkshireman thrust out his lip, which had a lump on it, and said, "What's that?" "That's cancer," said the doctor. "And what's to be done with it?" "Cut it out." "What's your fee?" "Two guineas." "You must make a deal of money at that rate." And so ended this highly parsimonious exchange in which the Yorkshireman gained the benefits of the sick role and the doctor two guineas.

The speed with which the sick role can be conferred is used to good dramatic effect in Dore Schary's play, *Sunrise at Campobello*. Franklin Roosevelt is first shown returning with his children from a swim in the frigid Canadian waters and then Indian wrestling with his son Jimmie. As he tells Eleanor how he longs to stay until Labor Day, he is suddenly seized with a pain in his back. He instantly denies that it is of any importance—"must be a spot of lumbago"—but shows by his fear that he is not so certain. Eleanor commands, "You get into bed. I'll bring you up a tray." To which F.D.R. meekly acquiesces. In a few lines, he is transformed from a tough, athletic young father—"undefeated and still champion"—to a sick man grateful to be sent to bed.

Some people who clearly need the sick role reject it. It is easy enough to see why: they hope that by rejecting the sick role, they can reject the illness as well. This is the case with Pavel Nicholayevich Rusanov in Solzhenitsyn's *Cancer Ward*. Pavel knows perfectly well that the ever-growing lump on his neck has put him in a cancer ward. What he cannot accept is the loss of his status—he is an important official—for he quickly discovers that cancer is a great equalizer. He finds himself in a ward with eight others, all of whom he regards as social inferiors. But a new status emerges: Pavel realizes with a shock that his is not one of the milder cases.

Like so many other hospital patients, Pavel especially resents being left to lie around and worry while the doctors are nowhere to be seen. He makes up his mind to pull rank when the doctor appears, "Comrade Dontsova, I shall be forced to inform the Ministry of Health of the way things are conducted at this clinic." When Dr. Dontsova explains that she has come to treat him he replies, "No. It's too late now."

But Pavel's threats melt into nothing as she asks him to stand, to move his head, to bend it forward. The examination is more eloquent than any words: he had lost practically all movement of his head. Pavel agrees that he will decide "tomorrow" whether to accept the treatment. Now Dontsova has him, "No, you must decide today."

"Couldn't it wait till Monday . . . ?" he bargains. This brings out Dontsova's Aesculapian authority:

Comrade Rusanov! You accused us of waiting eighteen hours before treating you. How can you suggest waiting seventy-two? Either we take you in for treatment or we don't. If it's yes, you will have your first injection at eleven o'clock this morning. If it's no, then you must sign to the effect that you refuse to accept our treatment and I'll have you discharged today. But we certainly don't have the right to keep you here for three days without doing anything. While I'm finishing my rounds in this room, please think it over and tell me what you've decided.

And so she moves on to the next patient, and the next. Finally Pavel's words ring through the ward, "Doctor, I give in. Inject me!"

Some people need the sick role but cannot get it for a variety of reasons. In Barbara Williams's children's book, *Albert's Toothache*, a toothless turtle-child named Albert complains that he cannot get out of bed because he has a toothache. This throws the family into confusion. His father argues, logically enough, that Albert cannot have a toothache because turtles do not have teeth. His brother boasts, "Who's afraid of a toothache?" His sister believes that he is a malingerer who is trying to get out of his responsibilities at home and at school. His mother, who is kindness itself, does not argue about the toothache, but she does not believe him either. She tries to coax him back to normalcy by offering him various treats—his favorite breakfast, a game of ball, and finally, the family snapshot album with pictures of them all in Disneyland. His mother's determined but misplaced

kindness moves Albert beyond complaining, and he is reduced to tears. Then Grandmother Turtle arrives, and starting with the premise that Albert is telling the truth, she soon
sets things straight. She asks, *"Where* do you have a toothache?"* and Albert shows her his toe, bitten by a gopher into
whose hole he stepped. Grandmother then wraps her hand-
kerchief around the "toothache," and Albert, smiling, gets
out of bed.

This simple story is very helpful in showing the consequences of being refused the sick role. Albert behaves badly
with his undiagnosed "toothache," and his family's efforts to
reinstate him in his normal role are to no avail. Albert's
morale reaches its lowest point when his mother produces
the family photograph album: extreme kindness in the absence of the sick role is harder to bear than sternness. Albert's father is stern, which might have given Albert the option of believing he feels miserable because his father is
unsympathetic. However, his mother's kindness rules out
that possibility, and since Albert's analytical powers are
small, he is now miserable, apparently, *for no reason.* And
that is worse than the original pain. However, when Albert's
grandmother installs him in the sick role his first action is *to
get out of bed.* Far from pushing him toward invalidism, the
sick role helps him to rally his moral forces and behave as
normally as the injury allows. Without the sick role he sulked
and whined in bed. A sick person without the sick role is
rather like the man without a country. He is on his way to
becoming what the Anglo-Saxons called a "nithing," a person without a role.

In 1969, a story in the *Trentonian* revealed the plight of a
750-pound New Jersey man who begged the county officials
to hospitalize him. "I can't go on like this," he wept. Unem-
ployable because of his appearance, Mr. Chasse had been on
the county welfare rolls. A county physician took the view
that Mr. Chasse was eating himself to death and would not
live much longer unless he mended his ways. However, a

private physician who had been treating Mr. Chasse backed up his patient's contention that he ate only two meals a day and that overeating was not the source of his difficulties. Without the sick role, Mr. Chasse was seen as an exceptionally self-indulgent glutton; with the sick role, he was seen as a very ill man, requiring immediate treatment. Both the life and the moral standing of this poor man were at stake as he begged for the sick role.

For a person who needs the sick role, there is nothing worse than to be told by a series of medical specialists that nothing abnormal can be found. This was the experience of a woman whom medical writer Berton Roueché described in his story, "Impression: Essentially Normal." Mrs. Morton's illness began with the sensation that her apartment house or office building was being given a sudden shake. At first she thought the two buildings, both old, were settling, but the appearance of many new symptoms soon convinced her that the problem did not lie in the buildings but in herself. Her whole sense of spatial relations began to fall apart, and she found herself living in a sort of Hall of Mirrors, a fun-house that wasn't funny. Floors and walls were sinking and rising unpredictably, streets and buildings were tilting and swaying. Yet none of the doctors whom she consulted could find anything wrong. She says, " 'Impression: essentially normal.' It sounds so reassuring. . . . So comforting. But it isn't. . . . It was terrifying. While I hadn't the vaguest idea of its medical meaning, I was sure of one thing. It couldn't mean that I was normal at all, because I wasn't. I was just the reverse. I became convinced it meant I was miserably sick and nobody had the faintest idea why." At last, Mrs. Morton's illness was diagnosed; she was told that she had labyrinthitis or Ménière's syndrome, a disorder ot the middle ear causing disequilibrium. In spite of the fact that Mrs. Morton had come to believe that she was doomed or dying, what impressed her about the diagnosis was not that the condition was benign and probably self-limiting, but, as she said,

"What left me simply weak with relief was knowing the truth at last. My trouble was no longer a mystery. At least it had a name. It was astonishing what a difference that made. And I wasn't alone. There were many other people in the same boat—thousands of them, apparently. Labyrinthitis is really quite common, I gathered. Or, rather, I made it my business to find out." While we all wish to be treated as individuals, no one wants to have a unique disease. One of the functions of the sick role is to put that sick person "in the same boat" with other people. To name a disease means that others have it (or else it would have no name), that something is known about it, and that there are doctors experienced in treating it. It also means that the patient has the responsibility of learning about the illness.

In an incident reported by Dr. Joseph Cardamone in *Modern Medicine* magazine, a young doctor asked a more experienced consultant, "How do you deal with a goldbrick?" The patient in question was a twenty-two-year-old man, in apparently good health, whose boss had threatened to fire him unless he "shaped up" or proved that he had a medical problem. The young man's only complaint was "intermittent weakness." The young doctor was prejudiced by the boss's estimate of the young man as a malingerer, and it took many searching questions by the consultant to show that there were other possibilities. After a more careful examination, the young doctor said, "His history may be a little better for organic illness than I originally perceived." This proved to be an understatement. The consultant summed up the case, "I'm afraid that with a cardiomyopathy associated with a skeletal myopathy [heart and muscle diseases] this young man may not survive for a very long time. . . ." From the patient's point of view, it is surely better to be a malingerer than to have a probably fatal illness. Yet so strong is the morality of medicine that the young doctor clearly implies that it is better to have a diagnosis of a terrible disease than to be accused of being a malingerer. Had the young man died without benefit of a diagnosis, he would not have been the first "malingerer" to have had the sick role conferred upon him when on the autopsy table.

Is there anything worse than dying a malingerer and receiving the sick role posthumously? Yes! It is the situation of the parents of babies who die of what is now called sudden infant death syndrome or S.I.D.S. This is an illness with no known pathology and a one hundred percent fatality. A previously healthy infant, usually between three weeks and six months of age, is simply found dead. Since the child was never sick the parents do not get the blame-free benefits of the sick role. Instead, they often blame themselves and have sometimes been accused by members of their families, the police, and doctors of causing the child's death. In self-defense, these unlucky parents have banded together to form the National Foundation for Sudden Infant Death. One member, Adrienne Walsh, in an article appearing in the *Birmingham Post-Herald*, wrote, "Parents should be encouraged to approve an autopsy of the infant to rule out congenital defects, the presence of some other disease, or just to prove the death did not result from giving the baby the wrong food." While the autopsies may lead to some useful clues as to the cause of the illness, their most obvious value is the retroactive conferral of the sick role and, with it, the removal of blame from the parents.

Far more frequent are those illnesses for which tests are sometimes inconclusive or whose symptoms may initially be confused with psychological problems. A political science student at a university found himself suffering from increasing fatigue, sleepiness, and chills. The condition grew steadily worse until he had to sleep as much as twenty hours a day and felt warm only when wrapped in eight blankets. He went to his student health service and was told that there was nothing physically wrong with him; he had psychological problems and needed psychotherapy. He did not find this advice at all convincing or helpful and so went instead to procure some books from the medical library. Wrapped in his blankets, he read on until he determined that he had hypothyroidism. He then consulted a local practitioner who confirmed the diagnosis, installed him in the sick role, and treated him successfully.

A particularly appalling account of the failure to confer the sick role is told by a surgeon, Dr. I. S. Cooper, in his book *The Victim Is Always the Same*. Dr. Cooper treats children who have a dreadful disease called dystonia musculorum deformans, in which the child's limbs gradually contort like corkscrews, leaving the victim in an agonizingly painful invalidism interrupted only by death. Dr. Cooper has developed an elegant and difficult brain operation, a form of cryosurgery, which has enabled him to restore many of the victims of this grotesque disease. He tells the story of three of his young patients: Susan, Janet, and David. What they had in common besides dystonia was that they were treated by psychoanalytic methods, thus delaying their eventual diagnosis and treatment while causing the greatest amount of blame, guilt, and emotional suffering to their families. These miserably ill children were seen as showing provocative, masochistic, and exhibitionistic behavior; all were said to have conversion hysteria.* Psychodrama and other analytic treatments in Susan's family drove her parents to the brink of divorce. Susan's mother became so depressed that she considered suicide; she even had an illegal abortion because she felt she was unfit to be a mother. Meanwhile, Susan's father had a vasectomy. One night, when Susan's symptoms of spasms and twisting were unusually severe, her mother called their pediatrician. He agreed to write a prescription, but added the warning, "you people better solve your problems in that household." When Susan's parents took her to a state psychi-

---

*Hysterical neurosis, conversion type: symptoms of physical illness that are not caused by such illness, such as paralysis or loss of hearing. The symptoms usually symbolize a conflict and involve portions of the body innervated by sensory or motor nerves.

atric clinic, the admitting psychiatrist remarked, "There is nothing wrong with this child, she is the most stable kid I have ever met." It was this psychiatrist who started Susan on the path that eventually led to Dr. Cooper and treatment.

When Janet saw Dr. Cooper she told him that she had been locked in a bare room for three months and had to crawl along the floor to get her food, which was left just inside the door. Janet said that her psychiatrist told her that she was "wacky—up here in my noggin." To which the intrepid Janet replied, "Phooey!"

David had had 146 therapeutic sessions while at a mental hospital. His peculiar gait, which caused his trunk to move backward and forward, was interpreted as a fear of touching his own penis. At the end of the discharge report David's therapist noted, "It seems he wasn't at all ready to give up his symptoms yet because they were giving him too much gratification to be relinquished."

Dr. Cooper, compassionate man that he is, does his best to see these psychiatric atrocities as simply cases of misdiagnosis, which can always happen in medicine. Aesculapian authority does not mean and has never meant that doctors are infallible. They try things and see if they work. If a treatment does not work they try something else, attempting to correct their course by the nature of the previous response. This is the "dialogue between the possible and the actual" which Peter Medawar, in *Induction and Intuition in Scientific Thought*, said was the basis of scientific reasoning. It requires not only that the doctor observe how the patient is doing, but that he listen to what the patient says.

In spite of the reputation that psychiatrists have acquired for "just listening," some of them seem to do anything *but* listen. Janet's mother complained, "The psychiatrist looked at her for five minutes and asked, 'How come this child hippity-hops?' That made me mad because this is all he did—five minutes and he labeled her a conversion hysteric on such a short evaluation—after he'd talked to her, I'd say, for a few minutes in a room." Had this psychiatrist been willing to listen he might have learned, among other things, that Janet's mother had a tremor in her right hand which she suspected (and Dr. Cooper confirmed) was related to Janet's illness.

Dr. Dolittle has a special place in the world of fictional doctor-heroes because he took the trouble to learn the language of the animals he treated. The plow horse says to him, "You know, the trouble is, sir . . . the trouble is that *anybody* thinks he can doctor animals—just because animals don't complain. As a matter of fact, it takes a much cleverer man to be a really good animal-doctor than it does to be a good people's doctor."* Now what does one make of doctors whose patients *can* talk but who don't bother to listen to what those patients say?

What the sick person wants above all else is to be believed. As Grandmother Turtle put it, "The trouble with all of you is that you never believe him." Even if the prognosis is abysmal, treatments ineffectual, diagnosis terrifying, even if there is no diagnosis at all, the sick person needs to have his experience of himself confirmed. The one thing we are sure of in this unsure world is that we experience what we experience. The doctor may have—perhaps, does have—a better explanation than the patient as to why he feels so ill, but the patient himself is the best judge, indeed the only judge, of whether or not his body feels ill. It is simply not possible to practice clinical medicine unless one is prepared to assume that the patient comes to the doctor in good faith, to relate as best he can where it hurts, what he is experiencing.

Charles Darwin was fortunate in having as his doctor Sir Andrew Clark, who treated him in a kind and encouraging manner even though it was not possible to diagnose Darwin's illness. Darwin suffered from lassitude, gastrointestinal discomfort, and heart trouble and was a semi-invalid for the remainder of his life after the famous voyage of the *Beagle*.

---

*Hugh Lofting, *The Story of Dr. Dolittle*.

He knew many people thought him a hypochondriac and in *Charles Darwin*, by Sir Gavin de Beer, we learn of a letter he wrote gratefully to his friend Hooker, "every one tells me that I look quite blooming and beautiful; and most people think I am shamming, but you have never been one of those." It now seems likely that Darwin had Chagas' disease, which is caused by a trypanosome carried by the South American benchuca bug. Darwin wrote about being bitten by this bug on March 25, 1834, but the bug was not known to be the carrier of Chagas' disease until 1909, twenty-seven years after Darwin's death.

Sometimes, we do not know how often, a person known to have a serious illness refuses to accept the sick role even though he knows his life may thereby be shortened. A famous example of this is D. H. Lawrence, who had tuberculosis but characteristically never admitted it; he referred to it as bronchitis or the flu or a cold, usually blaming the particular place he happened to be staying. In *D. H. Lawrence*, his friend and biographer, Richard Aldington, writes, "Nobody can say he was wrong to do this. Even from a medical point of view it might have been of psychological benefit, provided he had taken the necessary physical precautions. His comparative neglect of them may have been due to ignorance, but far more to an instinctive belief that better a short full life than the quarter-life of a permanent invalid prolonged to seventy." Yet perhaps a doctor very adroit in the use of Aesculapian authority might have inspired this exceptionally difficult patient. If Lawrence viewed his illness as a heroic struggle he might have had the benefits of the sick role without giving up his fierce independence and his genius for life. We can only be grateful that Solzhenitsyn found the courage to accept the sick role for his cancer and then gave us *Cancer Ward*, one of the two great novels of the sick role (the other being Thomas Mann's *The Magic Mountain*), as well as his later works.

Since doctors are fallible, we may be certain that the sick

role is sometimes conferred by mistake. But it does not matter very much unless it is accepted by mistake. How often this mutual error occurs is very hard to establish since it is difficult to prove that someone is *not* ill. If a person feels ill, says he is ill, and wants to be treated, and if the doctor finds his complaints plausible, the sick role may be conferred and treatment undertaken. The best defense against a mistaken conferral of the sick role is a well-informed patient who is on good terms with his body and has some instinct about whether or not he is in need of medical attention. The sick role cannot be conferred by force and doctor's orders are really only advice. However, there are emergency situations in which the decision to treat must be made by someone other than the sick person; there is no way of getting agreement about the sick role from someone who is totally unconscious, too young to speak, or in a toxic brain state. But these situations are usually temporary, even in psychiatry, and do not constitute the bulk of medical decision-making.

The sick role is a valuable human resource; its proper use and preservation are the responsibility of all of us as patients and potential patients. We must not damage it by malingering, by allowing ourselves to lapse into invalidism, or by failing to accept it graciously when it is needed. We must not allow doctors to damage it, however unwittingly, by medical arrogance, by pseudoscientific pretensions, or by bumptious bad manners. We must not permit them to fall back on their ancient priestly role and deliver moralizing sermons to us when what we need is medical advice. Malpractice suits damage the sick role; we must find a better way to guard it. Like fossil fuel, the sick role is an inheritance which we have long taken for granted and used cavalierly, but now we must seriously learn about it in order to preserve its benefits and pass them along to our children.

IV *Swanelo*

Do PATIENTS HAVE RIGHTS? Almost anyone would agree they do, but it has been left to a committee of the American Hospital Association to produce a bill of rights for patients. Of this document, Lawrence K. Altman, in an article for the *New York Times*, wrote, "The expectation that many nurses and aides will hand such a document to patients as they enter the hospital is a revolutionary step for medical centers, which have been under fire from many critics of the health system."

A bill of rights is normally written by a group of people who feel they have been deprived of their rights. It is formulated with reference to the parties that have already or might in the future deprive them of the rights which they seek to enjoy. Thus we would think it strange if we read in our history books that our Bill of Rights was handed to us by King George III or that the Magna Carta was prepared by King John for the benefit of his grateful barons. We find it equally strange that the present bill of rights for patients, although commendable in its object, was not the result of efforts on the part of patients' groups nor was it the result of negotiations with doctors or possibly nurses. Instead, it was presented by a third party, an organization representing the administration of hospitals.

What then are patients' rights? It seems to us that those who conferred these particular rights upon patients were little concerned with exactly what rights people have when ill, but rather with obtaining legal protection for their own organization, the hospital, which by usage has been in the habit of removing or reducing people's rights and is now handing some of them back.

The only member of the American Hospital Association committee who cast a dissenting vote, Dr. Robert C. Long, expressed a fear that the bill of rights would be used as a legal, rather than as a moral document. As reported by Barbara Yuncker in the *New York Post*, Dr. Long asked, "Why not give each patient a list of the ten most-likely-to-be-successful law suits against hospitals?" He was inferring that while a patient without rights might be a nithing (that is, a person without a role), a patient with rights but no duties may well be a tyrant, in this case, a litigious tyrant.

How is it that we have come to think of rights as being separable from duties? Duties seem to have played a small part in the Jeffersonian cosmos; Thomas Paine, the author of *The Rights of Man*, and the writers of the Constitution and the Bill of Rights were preoccupied with the spectre of absolute monarchy in which the monarch's rights are total and the people have nothing but duties. As the writers of the Constitution saw it, by assigning rights to all, this great imbalance would be automatically repaired. Perhaps they assumed that men of principle would always be ready to undertake their appropriate duties and that it would always be obvious what those duties were and how they ought to be performed.

Lawyers seem more aware than doctors or patients that there can be no rights without duties. In answering the question "Is a lawyer obligated to defend a Mafia killer or a corrupt politician?" Edward Bennett Williams said, according to Donald Robinson in the *Birmingham News,* "Now, there can be no rights without correlative duties. If someone has the right to counsel, then lawyers have a duty to respect that right. I construe this to mean that lawyers are obligated to give help to those who seek it."

The split between rights and duties is reflected in our language, for if one looks up rights in the dictionary, one is not referred to duties, and if one looks up duties, one is not referred to rights. However, the Barotse, a Bantu people, have a single word which means the concept of rights *and* duties: *swanelo.* Max Gluckman, whose study of the Barotse law appears in Alan Dundas's *Everyman His Way,* wrote, "So they can make a 'right' into a 'duty.' It is, formally, bad logic, but it may be brilliant judicial logic." The Barotse, then, would not have a Bill of Rights, but a Bill of *Swanelo.* Their language requires a delicately balanced and highly dynamic reciprocity of rights and duties while our language is non-reciprocal in this respect and so we frequently act as if rights and duties existed in isolation from each other. It is not so clear in our de-tribalized society that one man's right is another man's duty.

We once heard a story about a free medical clinic which serves young people who have small incomes. One day a man drove up to the clinic with a truckload of furniture he wished to donate to the clinic to make it a pleasanter place. He asked a number of young people who were standing outside the clinic to help him unload the furniture, but they refused. He unloaded the truck himself while they watched. This made him very angry, but he had no words to express why it felt so wrong to him. Being a man of feeling he was sensitive to the moral climate and knew that, somehow, things were worse rather than better as a result of his efforts.

He felt intuitively that since he had increased their rights by trying to make the clinic pleasanter and more comfortable, their duties should also have increased: in other words, there should have been an increase in *swanelo*. In fact, there was a decrease in *swanelo*, since the gap between rights and duties had widened, not narrowed.

A possible explanation for this situation is that the free clinic had been "given" to these young people as a privilege rather than as a right, just as the patients' bill of rights had been given to patients by those who had no right to withhold them in the first place. Privileges are not the same as rights because they can be withheld at the whim of those bestowing them. They do not call forth an increase in duties.

Robert Massie, writing about his son Bobby's hemophilia, bitterly resented having to beg people for donations of blood. He was made to feel that this was a privilege, but because the United States is a rich country which takes great pride in its public health and medical services he felt that it ought to be a right. When the Massie family later moved to France Bobby was fully covered by insurance for his many transfusions; what had been a privilege in the United States was a right in France.

The Massies had every reason to demand their rights, for not only had they shown themselves to be responsible partners in the long and bitter fight for Bobby's life, but they had proven to be exemplary and innovative team members. They constantly found new duties to perform on Bobby's behalf, such as rigging an intercom system so that he could participate in school lessons while at home in bed; reading and studying about hemophilia; maintaining excellent relations with the doctors upon whose skill and cooperation Bobby's life depended; arranging for summers in Maine where Bobby could have a more normal social life among people who did not reject suffering or handicap; teaching Bobby to triumph over periods of intense pain; and writing two books on hemophilia, *Nicholas and Alexandra* and *Journey*, which have served to alert the general public to the unsolved problem of this terrible and disruptive disease. They felt entitled to new rights because they had demonstrated their willingness to undertake new duties.

Perhaps the most important duty the Massies undertook was teaching Bobby about his illness. Bobby was shown microscope slides of his own blood. As a school project, he wrote a paper about his illness, including graphs he had made of his bleeding episodes over several months. As a young adult, he learned to transfuse himself, which allowed him to travel alone and to enroll at Princeton University as an undergraduate.

In learning to transfuse himself, Bobby has done more than make his life and that of his parents more convenient. He made his life safer, for only Bobby has the inside information deriving from his own acute self-observation which tells him when a transfusion is needed. In *Journey*, his father wrote, "Bobby transfuses himself less often, using less concentrate than before. The reason is that he can be precise: he better than anyone knows what is happening inside his body and can choose the moment to act." Bobby has both the right and the duty to use his knowledge of his own reactions to better his chances of survival. Furthermore, since his self-observation and self-transfusion reduce the amount of concentrate he uses, more of this scarce, life-saving substance is left for other hemophiliacs.

Bobby has shown a keen understanding that it is his duty as a patient to sustain the morale of those trying to help him. When his father was first learning to transfuse him, Bobby cheered him on, saying, "Try again, Dad. It really doesn't hurt that much." In this way, he has been able to bring out the best in those on whom his life depends. He has done more than this, for he has come to see his devastating illness as an integral part of his own character development and so by being a highly responsible patient he has transcended the disadvantages of his illness to become a better and more enlightened human being—the ultimate triumph over an unlucky fate.

The high standard of *swanelo* among the Massies has not always been met by others. Suzanne Massie describes their first encounter with their fate:

> Suddenly a man entered. It was at last the long-awaited Eminence, "Doctor" himself. He was wearing a gray suit, and his eyes looked down at the floor as he hurriedly came in. There were no preliminaries. He announced, coldly and matter-of-factly, "The child has classic hemophilia. There will be compensations, you may be sure." And with these enigmatic words, he turned on his heel and walked out.

Suzanne, her mother, and Bob Massie were left to weep, helpless and alone. *Swanelo* had fallen to zero.

The best indicator of high *swanelo* is high morale. High morale occurs when each person in a joint enterprise gets his rights and performs his duties, when all concerned are doing their best to fulfill their function, and all are in agreement about the object of the enterprise. This concept is graphically depicted in the television program, "M.A.S.H.," where the wounded soldiers want desperately to live and the intrepid doctors want desperately to save them. So high is the *swanelo* in these episodes that they are shown as peak experiences, never-to-be-forgotten moments which can rarely be equalled in more ordinary circumstances. The *swanelo* about the Korean War, however, is extremely low, since there is no such agreement about its worth. The doctors are often shown as depressed and demoralized when they stop taking care of their patients and ask themselves what they are all doing fighting a war in Korea.

Rose Levit and her daughter, Ellen, were successful in raising the *swanelo* between themselves and Ellen's surgeon. In *Ellen: A Short Life Long Remembered*, Mrs. Levit, relates taking her fatally ill daughter in for a doctor's appointment:

Ellen and I dragged ourselves into San Francisco for our appointment with Dr. Kramer. He was radiating pre-holiday cheer, but as always, his examination of Ellen was impersonal and cursory. It suddenly seemed important to Ellen and me that we talk with him, right there and then, about Ellen's illness and her feelings about it. It was important that he know how we felt about him. It was a painful confrontation; we made it clear that we saw his methods as impersonal and cool, though not unkind, that he seemed focused on his own schedule rather than on the patient's needs—and therefore his attitude was depersonalizing to Ellen.

The doctor listened. It seemed to us that he really listened. . . ."

After that confrontation the *swanelo* between Ellen, her mother, and the doctor, improved.

The mother of a schizophrenic boy found his psychiatrist overbearing in his manner toward her. While she appreciated that he was an able man who wished to help her son, she needed his moral support in order to carry on in the face of her son's illness. The psychiatrist's response was, "I am not your father." But there was no reason to believe that she entertained this delusion. She believed that as the mother of a sick boy she had the right to moral support from the doctor and that the psychiatrist had the duty to give it. By phrasing his answer in psychoanalytic jargon, he showed that while he enjoyed the rights of Aesculapian authority, he did not feel obliged to undertake its duties. Perhaps this is the very definition of a shrink, a word coined by patients to denote physician psychiatrists (not lay psychotherapists) who use their Aesculapian authority to undertake non-medical activities such as moral reproval, exhortation, or even outright defamation of character.

In order to get the benefits of medicine, one must have a certain amount of faith in the *swanelo* of the doctor-patient relationship. As in all matters, some people err too far in one direction; others, in the opposite direction. Molière had a phrase for those whose faith was very low indeed: "impious in medicine." In *The Feast of the Statue* Sganarel tells Don

Juan that having disguised himself as a doctor, people take him for one and accept his prescriptions. Don Juan says, "And why not? Why should you not have the same privilege as all other physicians have? They've no more share in curing distempers than you have, and all their art is pure grimace. They only receive the honour of happy success, and you may take advantage as they do, of a patient's good luck, and find everything ascribed to your remedies that can ˙proceed either from the favour of chance or the force of nature." Sganarel asks, "How, sir, are you so impious in medicine?" To which Don Juan replies, "Tis one of the greatest errors of mankind."

At the other extreme, we heard of a lady in England who was told in no uncertain terms by her doctor that she was to go to bed and stay there until he returned. The doctor then went home and died. Several years later, another doctor, inquiring as to why the lady was bedridden, unearthed this story of excessive medical piety and set her on her feet again.

In Lofting's *The Story of Doctor Dolittle*, there is a difference of opinion about medical piety between the king of the lions and his queen. The king refuses to aid Dr. Dolittle in his efforts to control an epidemic among the animals. When Dr. Dolittle chides him and says that some day the lions may need his help, the king scoffs and says that lions are never in trouble—they *make* trouble. However, arriving home, he finds his wife with a sick cub. When he proudly tells her of his exchange with Dr. Dolittle, she flies into a rage, "You never *did* have a grain of sense! . . . All the animals from here to the Indian Ocean are talking about this wonderful man and how he can cure any kind of sickness and how kind he is—the only man in the world who can talk the language of the animals! And now, *now*— when we have a sick baby on our hands, you must go and offend him. You great booby! Nobody but a fool is ever rude to a *good* doctor."

The person without medical piety accepts neither the

rights nor the duties of the sick role; the person who is too
pious accepts the duties but does not demand the rights. The
person who demands the rights without accepting the duties
is a patient-tyrant. Perhaps the most famous such tyrant in
literature is Sheridan Whiteside in Moss Hart and George S.
Kaufman's *The Man Who Came to Dinner*. The Stanley family,
on whose icy steps Whiteside has slipped, hope that this
unexpected stay in their home will provide them with wonderful evenings discussing books and plays and hearing
about all the famous people the great man knows. He, however, has other ideas. In addition to suing them for $150,000,
he informs them that in order to carry on as usual with his
international literary career, he will need the exclusive use of
their telephone, a bedroom for his secretary, as well as the
use of their living room, dining room, and library. He also
orders them to use the back stairs so as not to disturb him or
his guests. The doctor, who ought to have quelled Whiteside
with a good dose of Aesculapian authority, succumbs to his
glamour and begs him to read *The Story of a Humble Practitioner, or Forty Years an Ohio Doctor*, which the great man
hands to his secretary for quick disposal. The poor Stanleys
are caught by Whiteside's demands as guest, patient, and
litigant; each time they attempt to respond appropriately to
one of these roles, he deftly shifts to another, thus utterly
frustrating their attempts to establish *swanelo*.

In England, a war hero named Cheshire set up his Cheshire Homes to care for lonely and isolated people, most of
them afflicted with chronic or incurable diseases. The staff
were there to serve them "as if they were in their own
homes." This was interpreted, in one Cheshire Home, to
mean that the staff had to do anything the residents wanted.
A volunteer wrote, "One old lady actually showed me her
stick the first time I went—not to threaten me—and said that
when she arrived some years back the then warden had told
her not to hesitate to use it on any of the staff if they did not
do as she wanted! She added she had actually flicked one or

two of the youngsters if she felt they weren't being as helpful as they should be." The intent of the homes was entirely benevolent, but because there was no understanding of the *swanelo* of the situation, the result was to create patient-tyrants.

In addition to the unpleasantness of caring for patient-tyrants, the lowered *swanelo* may be dangerous to their lives. One nurse told us that grumpy, demanding patients who insist on their rights but pay no attention to their duties are liable to be neglected or, at least, not receive the very best of treatment. If a doctor, for whatever reason, comes to view a patient as a tyrant, it can very easily prejudice his opinion of the patient and so impair his judgment about the illness. In matters of life and death, small errors can be very important; therefore, patients are ill advised to distort the *swanelo* of the relationship by being tyrannous.

Some patients seem to be aware of this danger. Dale Armstrong, a reporter and broadcaster hospitalized with myasthenia gravis, found that he was falling into tyrannical ways. He was so very ill that the nurses did not realize this. In *Hang In There,* he wrote, "And then something happened. What flipped the switch, he'd never know. Some star in the cosmos exploded and it came all clear to him what was happening. He was becoming a professional patient! He was becoming the sick body that *more* than accepts what is being done for it. He was demanding this attention as his due, as what he was entitled to by the very act of being ill. . . . Pull up, old son. . . . You're on the road that leads to the enjoyment of poor health, a road as dangerous as it is soppy. The patient must join the others in trying to help the patient."

If Dale Armstrong had allowed himself to demand as much attention as he wanted, instead of no more than he needed, he would have been on his way into the role of the invalid— someone with a real illness and a right to the sick role. Some of an invalid's duties are undertaken: taking the medicine, restricting normal activities. The failure of *swanelo* occurs because the patient is not trying to get well as fast as possible, but is instead trying to make a career out of being sick. Usually, invalids make great demands on others, but fail to keep up their own morale. When the invalid is at home the other members of the family can be seen creeping around, restricting their own normal activities, feeling somehow guilty and responsible for the illness even though they were not and could not have been its cause. They don't protest because the patient does have some real illness, but there is a feeling of uneasiness, a lack of morale. Family members caring for a sick person ought to have a sustaining feeling of pride from doing their job well, however physically and emotionally taxing it may be. Even in their darkest hours, the Massies knew they were doing the best they could to help Bobby survive and to increase his chances of a normal life. The absence of such a feeling should alert family members to a failure of *swanelo* and lead to a careful re-examination of the rights and duties of the people involved.

The art of patienthood lies in being medically prudent, which means steering a well-plumbed course between the Scylla of medical piety and the Charybdis of skepticism and self-treatment. As Henry More put it in a letter to Anne Conway in 1653, "But that I may not seem to have killed my self by my own private conceit I am resolv'd to take Physick when emergencyes require, that I may fall with creditt." One cannot take a rigid stance, but rather, one must engage in a continuous dialogue between oneself and the doctor, between oneself and oneself: "How much can I expect from the treatment this doctor has to offer? How much will be demanded of me? Am I willing to carry out my part of the bargain? Does this doctor have my best interests at heart? Is he a good doctor? How much is known about my illness? Am I better not to treat it at all? Am I prepared to live with myself if I don't treat it and it gets worse? Am I prepared to live with myself if I *do* treat it and it gets worse? What price am I willing to pay for putting myself in this doctor's hands? If I feel things are going badly, or I have had enough, will he listen?"

Just such a dialogue goes on in Solzhenitsyn's *Cancer Ward* between the patient, Kostoglotov, and Dr. Dontsova. Kostoglotov is the kind of patient who *must* know what is happening to him, so he wangles a book on tumors out of Zoya the nurse—even though this is strictly forbidden. Kostoglotov wants Dr. Dontsova to tell him when he will be discharged. She replies that she has only begun to treat him. He explains to her that he does not aim at a complete cure, that he is grateful for his improved state of health, and now he wants to go home and enjoy it. He does not want to pay too high a price for the hope of life in the future; he will depend on his body's natural defenses. To which Dontsova replies, "You and your natural defenses came crawling into this clinic on all fours." Then Kostoglotov expresses the fear that she is really only interested in this treatment as an experiment, to see how it turns out, whereas he only wants to live in peace, if only for a year.

When Kostoglotov undergoes X-ray treatment from Dr. Gangart, he tries to discover the theory behind it. He cannot give himself to the treatment until he has grasped it for himself and so is able to believe in it. He tells her, "Don't be afraid, just explain. . . . I'm like an intelligent soldier who has to understand his mission before he'll fight." And so she yields and explains it to him. This increases the *swanelo* of the situation, since he is willing to do more if he is given more information: more rights lead to more duties.

Kostoglotov comes to trust Dontsova more because she is able to trace exactly where his tumor lies, "Only the patient can judge whether the doctor understands the tumor correctly with his fingers." However, he continues to argue with her that he does not want to be saved at any price, that he is satisfied with his degree of recovery. He argues that while he will accept the X-ray treatment, he will not accept the blood transfusions; he has seen bad reactions in other patients. She counters that the X-ray treatment is impossible without the transfusions. "Then don't give it!" he roars. "Why do you assume that you have the right to decide for someone else? Don't you agree it's a terrifying right that rarely leads to good? You should be careful. No one is entitled to it, not even doctors."

"But doctors *are* entitled to that right—doctors above all." Now, really angry, she says, "Without that right there could be no such thing as medicine!"

Dontsova decides to use shock tactics: she tells Kostoglotov that he is going to die. She offers to discharge him. He bargains: five or ten treatments, some reasonable number. . . . "Not five or ten! Either no sessions at all or else as many as are necessary! That means from today, two sessions daily instead of one, and all the requisite treatment. And no smoking. And one more essential condition: you must accept the treatment not just with faith but with *joy!* That's the only way you'll ever recover!" Kostoglotov accepts, but he does not tell her that he has something in reserve—a secret medicinal root from the woods with which he is planning to treat himself, or, if that fails, to kill himself. And so they battle on, like an old married couple, pleading, coaxing, exhorting, threatening, lying, making up. Neither of them knows that Dontsova, too, has cancer, and that she, too, will go through the same process as Kostoglotov, this time as a patient.

Both doctors and patients feel they deserve more rights now than in the past, and they are correct. Doctors are able to give much better medical care, at least in some respects, than ever before, and they want to be appreciated for this. Patients are better informed about medical matters and about their own physiology than ever before, and they want to be respected for this. Yet if either succeeds in increasing his rights without increasing the correlative duties, both parties will be left dissatisfied, disillusioned, and sometimes very angry. What is wanted is not just an increase in rights, but an increase in *swanelo*, in the reciprocity of rights and duties. Where *swanelo* is present, one sees the high morale that has always characterized the medical enterprise at its best. Human beings can face up to the most dreadful diseases, the most unlucky fates, if they carry out their duties and are given their rights—if they are not allowed to become nithings.

Patients

V *Patients by Themselves*

THE BEST THING is not to get sick, but what if you do? What
kind of patient will you make? A skillful, adroit patient who
gets the best from his medical advisors and his family while
maintaining his dignity and self-respect? Or a complaining
bungler who alienates those trying to help him, loses his
cool, and endangers his own life with histrionics? Illness may
rain down on the just and the unjust alike, but good patienthood can be learned and bad patienthood is an avoidable evil.

The most important thing a patient needs to know is how
experienced he is. Novice patients will have to learn everything at once, and, as with all roles, some will prove naturally gifted while others will have to have everything spelled
out for them. Experienced patients would do well to review
their past performance and decide whether they were successful patients or not; if not, they, like the novice patients,
will have to exert themselves to gain the necessary skills.

If illness strikes, the person's first duty is *to notice he is ill*. People vary tremendously in their ability to do this. Some are so attuned to their bodies, the slightest hint of malfunction alerts them to the possibility of illness. "What's this?" they say to themselves. "Something doesn't feel right (or look right, sound right, taste right, or smell right)." This automatic monitoring process works well in preventing illnesses and catching them early; the body's owner actually *knows* something about his body and about illnesses.

Other people have no automatic monitoring system and may notice nothing unless they are standing in a pool of blood or have a lump the size of a grapefruit. Or, they may suffer from symptoms for years without realizing that this means they are ill and ought to do something about it. If one has an untreatable illness, a capacity for suffering in silence may be a great blessing, but in treatable illnesses the same quality may be a handicap. This kind of person does not experience body and mind as being separate—hence the difficulty of defining himself as ill. Such a person may learn to observe that his organism is in a bad state, his dreams have changed, his quests are blocked, or his aura has changed color. Psychic healers often seem to be of this type, and they heal not so much with specific medical information as by a kind of psychic radar which pinpoints the area of difficulty.

Those people who tend to live in their own heads are naturally quite surprised to find that other parts of their anatomy demand attention from time to time. When they finally notice their own bodies, they sometimes go to the other extreme and become hypochondriacs. However, they may make up for these failings by being exceptionally open-minded about new medical information. If something is seriously wrong, this is the type of person who never lacks the most up-to-date information. One young man, noticing that his illness was getting steadily worse, dashed around the medical libraries of New York City duplicating the literature on his illness, knowing that he would soon be too ill to gather new information. He probably saved his life in this manner.

Some people "somaticize"—emotional problems and life difficulties are translated into physical symptoms. They can vomit at will, become paralyzed in a trice, develop a rash or fever, swell up like a balloon, and so on. This group includes the hysterics whose existence inspired psychosomatic medicine. The danger in this approach to life is that people may not believe them when they really need medical attention, and they may not believe it themselves.

The sick person's second duty is *to signal he is ill.* Many people believe they have done this when they have not. Sitting miserably in a corner in great pain may not be seen as a signal that one is ill and wants help, but as a signal that one is sulky or ill-tempered for some unknown reason. To signal to other people that you are ill means actually saying, "I am ill and need your help" and noting whether you have been heard and whether other people are behaving appropriately in response. If the response you get is "That's nice, dear," you have not been heard.

The sick person's third duty is *to insist he is ill.* It won't do you any good to notice you are ill and signal you are ill if no one believes you. What does it mean to insist that you are ill? It means that you know, in your guts, in your heart, in your mind, or wherever it is you know things, that you are ill and you are so absolutely certain about it that anyone who claims to have a relationship with you must believe you or call you a liar. If you cannot insist you are ill when you are, it may cost you your life, a high price to pay for a lack of persuasiveness. And how persuasive you are may be derived from your family's history with regard to illness.

Some families regard illness as a part of life, to be taken in stride, to be coped with as best as possible. In such families it is fairly easy to signal that one is ill and insist on it. The family will respond by trying to assess how serious the illness is, whether it is an emergency, whether it can wait, and so on. No one will be blamed, and other family members will be told without fuss or fanfare.

Other families regard illness as a sign of disfavor from the gods, an indication that the family fortunes are about to decline. The ill person will have trouble insisting he is ill, for the family will stoutly deny it. When and if they finally yield, it will be only to blame the sick person for bringing misfortune down upon their heads or to beat their breasts and wonder what they did wrong that one of their members should be ill. Other members of the family will not be told the dreadful news and soon the whole family may be engaged in an elaborate series of lies and deceptions. The ill person is not likely to find any of this helpful.

Some people find it hard to insist that they are ill, even if they know it to be true, because they do not believe they have the right to be ill. They believe they must always be working, or getting on in life, or improving themselves, or they have some plan or program which does not include the possibility of ever being ill. They are only too happy to agree with the family or the doctor who says they are not really ill; they make themselves sicker by adding to the illness itself the burden of concealing it from themselves and others. Such people sometimes collapse after years of carrying on in the face of unacknowledged illness, and once they do collapse, they find it hard to get going again: they must conquer both the illness and their former attitude. Watch out for the person who says: "I can't get sick. I'm too busy." He will ignore a small illness until it becomes a big illness, and then treat himself badly about it.

If you have noticed you are ill, signaled you are ill, and insisted you are ill, the next task is to assess the kind of illness you are up against. Trivial or serious? Contagious or not? Probably recoverable or probably fatal? Immediate action required or plenty of time for information-gathering? Most of the time illnesses are not serious and will go away by themselves. It's the other times you have to worry about. If you and your family have no experience with really bad illnesses, get a number of other people's opinions fast and hope that they know more than you do. One call to a doctor may settle it: "Come right into the hospital and I'll meet you there." But often there are differences of opinion and three friends will tell you it's nothing while a fourth says: "My wife had that. Act at once."

At every point, if the illness allows it, you want to know: is this something I have to decide right now or can it wait until I have other opinions? If there is time, you want to try simple remedies before complicated ones, safe treatments before dangerous ones, and inexpensive treatments before expensive ones. One man, who had blinding headaches, had in desperation agreed to exploratory eye surgery. While awaiting the surgery, his wife suggested he try her over-the-counter nose drops, and these worked. He had sinusitis! Moral: try simple things first.

Medical treatment consists largely of giving drugs, which are really poisons given in small amounts. The reason we are willing to take these substances is that the illnesses are worse or seem worse than the drugs—although we often later learn that the drugs are worse than the illness. People differ greatly in their response to drugs, some being extremely drug-sensitive while others appear to be unmoved by doses that would fell an elephant. Where you have a choice, do not take drugs you know or suspect are bad for you. Ask your doctor if there are less dangerous alternatives.

Some people are only too happy to pour over the *Physician's Desk Reference* and may decide to take, in addition to what the doctor recommended, a number of other drugs, procured from other, unsuspecting doctors or the medicine chests of friends. This is a poor idea, since drugs are much more dangerous taken in combination than they are singly— they have strange effects on each other. Before turning your body into an experimental chemistry laboratory, you might decide whether you trust the doctor you have, and if so, limit yourself for the time being to what he prescribes. If you have complaints, tell him. If his response is not satisfactory or you decide that you do not trust him, for whatever reason, find another doctor, not another drug.

A patient does not have the right to expect that others will know exactly what he is feeling. Illness is an altered state of consciousness about which less is remembered, if the literature is to be believed, than about psychedelic trips. Aldous Huxley wrote *The Doors of Perception* about his first mescalin experience, but no one has written *The Doors of Pneumonia*. In fact, most of us have very little memory of illness once it is past, so we cannot even sympathize with our former selves. Amnesia about the illness state is clearly merciful—what if we could *really* remember!—but it makes it hard for us to learn anything from our past illnesses. One frequently ill observer, Virginia Woolf, in her essay "On Being Ill," had this to say about our amnesia:

Considering how common illness is, how tremendous the spiritual change that it brings, how astonishing, when the lights of health go down, the undiscovered countries that are then disclosed, what wastes and deserts of the soul a slight attack of influenza brings to view, what precipices and lawns sprinkled with bright flowers a little rise of temperature reveals, what ancient and obdurate oaks are uprooted in us by the act of sickness . . . when we think of this, as we are so often forced to think of it, it becomes strange indeed that illness has not taken its place with love and battle among the prime themes of literature. Novels, one would have thought, would have been devoted to influenza; epic poems to typhoid; odes to pneumonia; lyrics to toothache. But no . . . literature does its best to maintain that its concern is with the mind; that the body is a sheet of plain glass through which the soul looks straight and clear, and, save for one or two passions such as desire and greed, is null, and negligible and non-existent. On the contrary, the very opposite is true. All day, all night, the body intervenes; blunts or sharpens, colours or discolours, turns to wax in the warmth of June, hardens to tallow in the murk of February. The creature within can only gaze through the pane—smudged or rosy; it cannot separate off from the body like the sheath of a knife or the pod of a pea for a single instant; it must go through the whole unending procession of changes, heat and cold, comfort and discomfort, hunger and satisfaction, health and illness, until there comes the inevitable catastrophe; the body smashes itself to smithereens, and the soul (it is said) escapes. But of all this daily drama of the body there is no record.

The fact that illness affects one's state of mind so much helps to explain why people are notoriously irrational about being sick and following medical advice. The doctor's view is that the patient has been told what to do and should do it and that's that. It rarely works out that way, and patients comply with doctor's orders even less—much less—than doctors suppose. An illness is a psychological and spiritual as well as physical event in the patient's life, not just a history, some test results, and prescriptions that lie in a folder in the doctor's office. If the illness is serious enough, it may change the person's whole life, alter his most important relationships, turn his personal philosophy upside-down, give him a new career. A well person's sick counterpart is a kind of *doppelgänger* who must be dealt with almost as a separate person. What kind of relation will the two have? Will it be a Jekyll-and-Hyde relationship in which one has no memory of the other? Will the sick person gradually take over the well one and shape his life? Will the well person force the sick one to yield up valuable clues about the whole person? Will the sick person force his well counterpart to take a closer look at human suffering, to develop compassion and tenderness where there was none? A patient concerned with these momentous issues may forget to have the doctor's prescription filled or he may take the pills twice and then misplace them.

A patient asks for medical help because, presumably, he wants to get well. Therefore it comes as a surprise that many patients have deep conflicts about whether or not they want to get well. Every conflict a person has ever had about being self-sufficient or being dependent, about making his way in the world or spending more time in fantasy or self-explora- tion, will surface during a long illness. Thus do patients sab- otage their doctor's orders and their own wish to get well. The doctor's authority, great as it is, is helpless against the infinite possibilities of mischief which the patient has avail- able to him twenty-four hours a day. That is why faith healers make so much of the patient's commitment to get well. The patient who has made a real commitment to getting well has greatly improved his chances, whatever the medical treatment, while the patient who remains ambivalent may fail to get well even with the best medical advice in the world.

Almost anyone can bumble through a short, acute illness, but it takes a real patienthood expert to manage a chronic ill- ness. Some chronic illnesses develop very slowly over a long period of time, perhaps with periods of remission in which it seems that one had imagined the whole thing. Alcoholism, schizophrenia, hypoglycemia, diabetes, non-convulsive epi- lepsy, hypothyroidism, multiple sclerosis, myasthenia gra- vis, cerebral allergy are all illnesses which make it difficult for the patient to carry out his first duty, to notice that he is ill. These illnesses also make it difficult to signal and insist that one is ill. The early symptoms are often confused with ordi- nary life problems or with psychological difficulties: fatigue, irritability, depression, loss of concentration. If you suspect that you have such an illness, give yourself the benefit of the doubt and try to talk with doctors who treat these illnesses, patients who have these illnesses, or doctors who are inter- ested in diagnostic puzzles. If all else fails, make a list of ev- erything you have that you suspect is a symptom, duplicate the list, and sent it to various doctors and to your friends and ask: does this sound like anything you are familiar with? Ei- ther somebody knows the answer to your question or you are in the same boat with a lot of other unhappy people with undiagnosed illness. It is most unlikely that you have a unique disease.

Sometimes another person with the same illness will recognize what you have. One woman who was constantly falling asleep at her job was told by a fellow employee, "I know what *you've* got; you've got hypothyroidism!" She knew, she said, because she had it herself. The sleepy woman didn't believe her. But then, at a routine insurance physical examination, the doctor noted that she had a very slow pulse and some other symptoms and he raised the possibility that she had hypothyroidism. This time she listened, sought treatment, and corrected the condition. She also lost many symptoms she did not even know were part of this illness. She had given up skiing because of cold intolerance, but now returned to it with pleasure.

What kind of marks would one give this woman for patienthood? She did not notice she was ill, signal she was ill, or insist she was ill. When her fellow employee told her she had hypothyroidism, she did not believe her. However, her willingness to listen to the doctor may have been greater because she had already been told once before. She was then willing to take corrective action. She can count herself lucky for these two chance encounters, for, left to her own devices, she might never have learned what she had. She cannot be given a very high mark for patienthood, but if she develops another illness, she may be more alert to her body's signals and more assertive about being ill.

The key to controlling many chronic illnesses is not medication (although that may be needed, too) but regimen. In Virginia Woolf's day, there was little that could be done medically for her schizophrenic illness, but a great deal that could be done to lessen the impact of the illness on her life. She and her husband, Leonard, learned that they had to carefully ration the amount of social and intellectual stimulation she could have, depending on how well or ill she was. The number of visitors, the amount of travel, the length of time she was permitted to work, all depended on their experience with what she could handle. This sensible plan allowed her many years of productive work and personal happiness. They knew very little about the illness itself, yet they managed better than many people who have schizophrenia today because they understood that the day-to-day regimen, which was their responsibility, was as important as anything the doctors could do for them. The Woolfs certainly get high marks for patienthood.

Another exemplary patient is John P. Darling, M.D. In his contribution to *When Doctors Are Patients* he tells his story. While training to become a surgeon, Darling developed epilepsy, probably as a result of a skull fracture. Rather than give up medicine, as he was advised to do, Dr. Darling changed his specialty to pathology. He began to conceive of himself as a wrestler pitted against an antagonist wrestler, his epileptic self. As the years passed, he learned to break the hold that the epileptic wrestler had upon him by learning to identify, evalutate, eliminate, or control the sources of strain that brought on convulsions. He found, for example, that simply getting up in the morning, the change in posture from lying to standing, could bring on a convulsion. He learned to eliminate these morning attacks by rising very gradually. Cold nights used to be followed by convulsions; these were conquered with the aid of an electric blanket. Severe, prolonged effort and unexpected demands proved to be a potent source of attacks, and, gradually, all this information was fed back into Dr. Darling's decision-making system. "Like good automobile drivers, I decelerate and accelerate slowly whenever I can," he said. He has learned to rest before meals, to eat slowly and not too much, and to limit fluid intake. The calendar and the clock are his best friends, for he has learned that he can expect regular increases in his tendency toward convulsions and thus be on his guard. Summing up his self-taught program, he said, "Each lesson I learned many ways, but finally well enough so that I do the right thing most of the time almost instinctively, instantly, accurately, and forcefully. It seems only natural to sense almost simultaneously most of the signs I show of predisposition to convulsion, even though minimal. These habits help my personal efficiency even when there is no danger of convulsion." Thus Dr. Darling has been able to carry on a full professional and personal life in spite of a major chronic illness, due almost entirely to his ingenuity in learning to defeat the antagonist wrestler. Dr. Darling gets full marks for his exemplary patienthood.

Dr. Darling believes that his habits help him "even when there is no danger of convulsion." He seems to be saying that his regimen for controlling his illness is also a good way to live. Indeed, anyone might benefit from a life free of excesses. Sick or well, we would all profit from a program which included, for example, no smoking, no overeating, little or no alcohol consumption, avoidance of junk foods, moderate exercise, staying away from known pollutants, and avoiding sexual promiscuity. While there are many illnesses and injuries which cannot be prevented that way (including Dr. Darling's skull fracture), some could, and we would certainly feel the better for it.

In any illness, whether there is a definitive treatment or not, there is always something the patient can do that makes it better and something that makes it worse. Except for a rapidly fatal illness, it is hard to imagine any illness in which nothing the patient did would make any difference. The patient's responsibility, then, is to take note of those things which improve his situation and do them more, to take note of those things which make it worse and stop doing them. While doctors can provide information and advice, and families can provide practical, emotional, and financial support, only the patient can make the thousands of little decisions which shape the course of the illness. It may very well be the patient's alertness, assertiveness, imaginativeness, and commitment to getting well which will determine the outcome of the illness.

When a patient has come through an illness he would be

well-advised to review for himself (before amnesia wipes the slate clean) how well he did as a patient and how his performance might have been improved. He might ask: how quick was I to notice I was ill? How successful was I in signaling I was ill? How insistent was I that I was really ill? How accurately did I assess the nature of the illness? How well did I make decisions about the safety and effectiveness of the treatments? How assertive was I about not making decisions faster than they had to be made? How compliant was I about following medical advice? How committed was I to getting well? How imaginative was I about discovering what helped and what hindered my recovery? How sensible was the regimen I maintained during the illness? How reasonable am I prepared to be about following a program that will keep me well?

A person who emerges from an illness having turned in a creditable performance as a patient has demonstrated that he possesses an essential social skill: he is an expert in patienthood. Many people today have all sorts of technical knowledge about computers, the international currency market, the workings of foreign automobiles, stereophonic systems, and so forth. Yet any of these experts might suddenly find himself ill and lacking even the most rudimentary ability to recognize that he is ill and say so. Doctors themselves are not immune from this possibility; the knowledge required is not taught in medical school. Anyone who masters the art of patienthood is not only fortified against such illnesses as fate may bring him in the course of his life, but he is a resource for all of us, those who have as yet escaped illness and those who have survived it in spite of our amateur status. Valuable as the sick role and Aesculapian authority may be, they are fully realized only in the presence of the adept, responsible patient.

VI *Patients and Doctors*

IF YOUR ILLNESS REQUIRES the services of a doctor and you know enough to get yourself one, you will then enter what for many people is one of the most difficult and frustrating of all human relationships. In addition to the inherent problem of not wanting to be sick and the irrational behavior which illness seems to induce in most of us, there is the doctor himself, a seemingly immovable yet unpredictable presence, fraught with hope and danger.

The doctor-patient relationship resembles that of the elephant and the mahout (the elephant driver). Elephants have many virtues: they are an excellent means of transportation in difficult country, and they can use their great strength to move heavy obstacles. They are not cheap to feed, but everyone knows that. All things being equal, one is lucky to have a good, strong, kindly elephant at one's disposal. However, for all their good nature, elephants are dangerous simply because of their size. They may sit, stand, or roll over on you quite inadvertently. Usually they don't do this, but once is enough. They sometimes urinate or defecate inconveniently and may squirt one playfully with water. These huge pachyderms are ordinarily friendly and considerate, but they are prone to acute attacks of panic which can be brought on by quite small creatures such as mice. Panicking elephants cannot avoid being a great nuisance. Now and again bulls of the species have attacks of "musth," a dangerous frenzy of sexual excitement; they then become savagely unpredictable and have to be restrained. A few elephants become rogues and seem to take pleasure in killing mahouts and non-mahouts, too. They should be recognized early and avoided.

Elephants are like doctors in that the very qualities which make them so useful—their power, strength, and sagacity—also make them dangerous. Patients are like mahouts, in that they need the elephants and can get essential services out of them, but they must learn how to manage them and how to avoid being trampled upon. They must also avoid stampeding them inadvertently.

The first thing a mahout must learn is to recognize an elephant when he sees one. All the expertise in the world will not help a mahout who has mistakenly mounted a hippopotamus or a rhinocerous instead of an elephant. Some mahouts who have failed to observe this precaution are no longer with us. For the same reason the patient must learn to recognize a clinical doctor who has Aesculapian authority and on no account try to get medical services out of a scientific investigator.

Once the mahout has found a real elephant, he must learn to train him properly. *Only mahouts can train elephants!* It might seem at first that the patient-mahout is negotiating from a position of appalling weakness and is therefore in no position to train the doctor-elephant. But the situation is not as bleak as it appears. While the doctor is always a doctor (even when sick, it appears), most people are patients only for short periods. When well, the sometime-patients can review their past performance, talk with others who have had the same illness or have seen the same doctor, and master the basic elements of patienthood. While doctors are impervious to blows, kicks, shouts, threats, and insults, which do not penetrate their elephantine hides, they are vulnerable to the patient who knows more about Aesculapian authority and the sick role than they do. Doctors like to have good patients, just as elephants like to have good mahouts, but many of them are too ignorant to get them except by chance.

Most exchanges between doctors and patients take place in the doctor's office. The first step in doctor-training is to make sure the doctor sees you at a time which bears some resemblance to your actual appointment. Of course, there are emergencies, but doctors can be taught to have their secretaries alert patients if there is unexpected surgery or some other delay. It is not beyond the wit of doctors and their office personnel to have a realistic flow of patients. One orthopedic surgeon was so poor at this that his patients not only had to wait as long as two hours to see him, but the low, soft office furniture that some decorator had provided for him made this wait torture for those with recent back operations. When at last admitted to the doctor's office, they were sternly advised to purchase special chairs, stools, and car seats to promote the healing of their injuries and on no account to sit on their usual furniture at home. Don't let your doctor play dumb about such matters; if he is moved neither by your comments, nor by tactful letters, ask some other doctor how to handle it and if nothing works, find yourself another doctor. No doctor is that much wiser or cleverer than another; it is only Aesculapian authority which makes the particular doctor you happen to be seeing appear so indispensable.

Assuming you have gotten in to see the doctor, you will now have the first actual exchange. You will try to tell him what's wrong; he will try to decide how serious it is and what can be done about it. You open the dialogue: "I've come to ask your advice. I have this lump (rash, pain, dizzi-

ness). . . ." So far, you have signaled that you are not putting yourself under his orders or asking him to take over
your life and make decisions for you, but only that you are
asking his expert medical advice. This will remind the doctor, in case he has forgotten, that what he gives is advice, not
orders. Then you are telling him you have noticed you are ill
and feel strongly enough about it to seek his help; you are
serious about correcting what ails you, but would naturally
be grateful if he can convince you there is nothing wrong,
that you have made a mistake, and can go home and forget
about it.

The doctor will then take a history and do a physical examination; he may order (i.e., advise) that you have some tests.
If the case is straightforward, the doctor may give advice on
the basis of this initial exchange. Then it is your turn to
gather information. You will want to know the name of the
illness you have, or at least its general category ("a virus").
You cannot be a responsible patient if you don't know what's
wrong with you. Neither Mrs. Morton with her labyrinthitis,
Albert Turtle with his "toothache," or Dr. Cooper's young
dystonia patients were in any position to act like responsible
patients until they learned what illness they were up against.

Once you have the name of your illness, you will want to
know what that name means in terms you can understand.
You will want to know the range or magnitude of what you
are dealing with, how serious it is, how treatable, how
urgently it must be treated, and so on. Then you will want
to know what your options are, for any illness can be treated
(or not treated) in a variety of ways. One woman, told that
she had breast cancer, wanted to know what her options
were. She was told that she might elect surgery, radiation
therapy, or chemotherapy (in that order) or, the doctor said,
"you can do nothing." The woman found it very comforting
to be offered the last alternative even though she decided
from the information given her that surgery would be her
best choice at that time. Being offered the possibility of

doing nothing reminded her she was only getting advice from the doctor, the decision about what to do was hers, and her enemy was the disease, not the doctor.

If you do not know what you have, you have no means and no occasion to compare yourself with others. Once you know the diagnosis, you can inquire about how bad a case you have compared to others with the same illness. Oddly enough, there is comfort in any of the possible answers. If you have the worst case ever seen, you can expect extra attention and comfort, perhaps even notoriety. This will also explain why you feel so bad and you won't have to accuse yourself of exaggerating. If you have a mild case of a bad disease, you can congratulate yourself on being spared a worse fate—and milder can be very relative! One woman in a polio ward congratulated herself for being the only patient who could breathe on her own *and* use her arms! If you have an average case of something, you can expect that the doctors will be familiar with your degree of the illness, and you will have the benefit of all the other average cases that have preceded you.

You may want to let the doctor know early in your relations with him just how experienced you are as a patient. You might say: "I want to be a cooperative patient, but I've always been so healthy I'm afraid I don't know much about it." Or "I don't know much about being ill or being a patient, so I'll need your help. Or "I'm the kind of person who needs quite a lot of information in order to be really cooperative." Or "I'm not used to making these kinds of decisions. I would like to go home and think about it. May I call you if I have further questions?"

If you are being advised to undertake a treatment which seems dangerous to you, you might say: "To be frank, this treatment scares me a little; I would feel more comfortable about it if I got the opinion of some other doctors. Would that be all right with you?" The wise doctor always encourages patients to get other opinions; he has everything to gain and nothing to lose by having a trusting, cooperative patient.

Suppose you agree to a particular treatment. You will want to be sure you have correctly understood what the doctor has ordered (advised). You may say: "Can you go over that again? I want to be sure I've got it right." Or "I have a very poor memory for details; I think I had better write down what you're saying." You may also say: "What can I do to help myself? Would my daily habits make any difference in the success of this treatment?"

Many people find, as they proceed with a medical treatment, that they accumulate questions which they are too nervous or embarrassed to ask when they see the doctor. You may say: "I tend to get nervous in a doctor's office, and I forget to ask what I want to know. Do you mind if I bring a list of questions?" Some doctors absolutely *hate* lists of questions, then you have to ask them to suggest how you can get your questions answered. Most doctors do best in face-to-face situations, some do well on the phone, others will answer questions in response to brief notes. The phone or the brief note are most useful if you have a single, specific question because then the doctor knows he does not have to commit much time to the answer. Be sure not to ask a lot of technical questions if you cannot make use of the answers. Not getting one's questions answered is such a common complaint among patients that it is worth your while to devote some energy to solving the problem with your particular doctor.

In the 1820s, a general improvement in the level of public information made patients eager to learn more about their illnesses. Matthew Baillie, president of the Royal College of Physicians, London, noticed this important social change and began to give his patients short, simple lectures about their illnesses. Before this time, doctors had prescribed and consoled, but rarely informed. But, Baillie's eulogist William Macmichael noted in *The Gold-Headed Cane*, ". . . as a more curious anxiety began to be observed on the part of the pa-

tient to learn everything connected with his complaint, aris-
ing naturally from the improved state of general knowledge,
a different conduct became necessary in the sick room. The
innovation required by the spirit of modern times never
could have been adopted by anyone more fitted by nature
and inclination to carry it into effect than by Dr. Baillie."
What Matthew Baillie had invented was the responsible patient, for the irresponsible patient has no need to know anything about his illness. Now that the level of general knowledge is higher than in Dr. Baillie's day, the *swanelo* of the
doctor-patient relationship must change accordingly. The
doctor has the duty to give more information than he has in
the past, the patient has the right to get more information
relevant to his illness. But then the patient has the duty to
use this information in order to be a more responsible patient, while the doctor has the right to expect that the information he gives will be used responsibly. If your doctor
balks at giving you the information you need, you must as-
sure him that this is not mere idle curiosity on your part, but
that you need it in order to carry out your part of the treatment effectively and intelligently. A doctor may prefer you
do as he says because he says it, but he is not likely to claim
that he prefers irresponsible patients.

Suppose none of the treatments for your particular illness
seem to be working, but you have heard about some new,
unorthodox treatment that you would like to try. And what if
your doctor panics? Doctors, like elephants, tend to stick
together and panic easily if you try to separate them from the
main herd. If you want your doctor to start rocking to and
fro, kicking up dirt, and trumpeting loudly, just tell him that
you want to try acupuncture, that you are also seeing a chiro-
practor, or that you would like to try coffee enemas or a
hypoglycemic diet. If you don't want to provoke what ele-
phantologists call a threat charge, don't tell him about these
things. Medicine, like all social institutions, has limits, and
at any given time, some things which are curative lie outside

its boundaries, although the passage of a few years may see them incorporated into the main body of medicine. If you wish to train your elephant, you must start with his natural repertoire of behavior, like any good animal trainer, and not try to get him to jump through hoops.

Another option for the patient in need of an innovative treatment is to find an elephant who is slightly separated from the main herd. While medicine as a craft is conservative, it does change—sometimes more rapidly than its practitioners admit—and so there are innovative and imaginative doctors around who will accept new ideas and try new treatments before their colleagues.

Sometimes doctors seem to be in solid agreement: a new treatment won't work or chiropractors are a menace. Other times, a patient may find that ten different doctors have ten different opinions as to what's wrong with him. It seems impossible at first to understand on what basis doctors agree with each other, on what basis they disagree. The answer lies in elephantology: doctors agree on whatever is or appears to be good for the herd and they are against anything that appears to damage the herd. Therefore they are against fringe practitioners and far-out treatments. Within the herd, what matters is the highly individualistic, sometimes idiosyncratic relation of each doctor to each patient. A doctor will give generous pain-killers to one patient and none to another; a patient will follow scrupulously the orders of one doctor and scarcely glance at those of another. Just because one mahout has taught his elephant to cross a rope bridge doesn't mean anyone else can do it!

Just as doctors are suspicious of new treatments and new kinds of practitioners, they are doubly suspicious of new illnesses. If you have the misfortune to have an illness which is not thoroughly familiar to doctors and thoroughly accepted by them, you are in for a very rough time. This is the occasion for the worst scenes that take place between doctors and patients. The patient goes in good faith to the doctor with his symptoms and his suffering; the doctor patiently goes through his paces, but he does not turn up anything that he recognizes as an illness. If he is a very good doctor, he will say: "I see that you are ill but I don't know what you have. Here are the names of some specialists who might be able to help you." If he is a not-so-good doctor, he will say: "I have tested you for various illnesses; the test results are negative; therefore you are *not* ill." If he is even worse, he will add: "It's all in your mind." Few things are as likely to evoke agitation, hostility, and indignation than denying someone the sick role. In no illness is denial of the sick role likely to help. If the doctor truly believes that someone is not ill but is simulating illness—malingering—then this calls for the most careful professional consideration. The possible consequences for the patient and his family may be serious, even fatal. Not only does it do harm, but it prevents the patient from making and being taught to make use of his own moral, intellectual, and spiritual resources. To make matters worse, the moral position of a doctor who devotes himself to detecting malingerers is much weaker than that of those who treat the sick.

The elephant's great strength is useful to us only if he is a moral elephant. If he cannot be trusted, if he runs amuck, if no mahout can train him, then he must be restrained or shot. And so it is with the doctor: his great strength, derived from Aesculapian authority, is useful to us only if he behaves morally, if he confers the sick role when appropriate, if he can be constrained by his patients' legitimate needs.

Elephants are so very large and mahouts are so very tiny; can the mahout really prevail against his elephant? Mr. Otis Simmons, a fifty-eight-year-old derelict, was brought into a New York hospital with frostbite on both legs. The doctors ordered his legs amputated. Mr. Simmons thought otherwise, "My two legs got to stay on. I won't have the operation," he said. "I got to cure my own self." As reported in the *New York Times*, the State Supreme Court upheld Mr.

Simmons's right to refuse amputation, and, with antibiotic treatment, he began to improve. Mr. Simmons did much better at standing up to his doctors than Howard Hughes did to his, but then Mr. Simmons was acting as a responsible patient, whereas Mr. Hughes was merely trying to make himself more comfortable.

The problem for most patients, especially those who have never been sick, is that they believe themselves to be well-trained mahouts riding well-trained elephants, when they are really more like visitors to African wildlife preserves getting their first look at wild elephants. Being ill is like mounting an elephant for the first time and learning mahouthood as you go along. Your chances of survival depend on how quickly you pick up the elements of mahouthood and on whether or not your elephant has been broken in by someone else. We must develop a tradition of patienthood in which the wisdom learned by some patients is passed along to those who come after. Gentle and expert goading from responsible patients will tame all but the wildest doctor.

The real mahout has a deep understanding of his elephants and demonstrates this by responsible mahouthood. Elephants respect this and will be devoted to their mahouts. Responsible patients are welcomed by good doctors who complain frequently about their patients' irresponsible ways. Apart from disapproving, doctors do little about their patients' bad behavior because they have little knowledge of their own authority and of the best ways to encourage better sick-role behavior.

The moral doctor finds it difficult to resist the proper, formal appeal of the moral patient. The trouble, now, is that this seldom happens because there are not as many well-trained patients about. Exemplary patienthood is becoming increasingly necessary if, amidst the gadgetry, patients are to maintain themselves as human beings. When the doctor had little in the way of medicine, equipment, tests, etc., the human qualities of the patient were obviously of central importance to the medical enterprise. Doctors paid attention to their patients because there were far fewer distractions. The patient, by being responsible and thus raising *swanelo*, can bring himself into focus in an appropriate and safe way. The doctor's authority and the patient's responsibility must balance at the highest possible level of *swanelo*. If the doctor and/or patient are inexperienced regarding the sick role, the *swanelo* will fall. Either the doctor's authority or the patient's responsibility will be damaged, and attempts to repair this damage are frequently worse than the initial harm done. The good, responsible patient has great advantages and may significantly better his chance of survival.

The key to controlling Aesculapian authority is a quiet but firm assertiveness on the part of the patient that this authority will be used for only one purpose: the betterment of the individual patient. It exists for no other purpose. It is not given to the doctor in order to make money, to seduce patients, to play God, to perform interesting experiments, to try out novel social schemes, to pass moral judgments, or to probe other people's psyches. It is given to him to preserve the life and ease the suffering of sick people, amongst whose number he will some day take his place.

VII *Patients in the Hospital*

A SICK PERSON AT HOME is like an animal in its natural habitat; a sick person in a hospital is like an animal in the zoo. At home, patient and family draw strength from being in their own territory, with its familiar surroundings and comforts. In the hospital, the patient lives in an alien and frightening environment, while the family skulks in the corridors, without a territory and so almost without a status. Why, then, do we move ourselves from home to hospital? Only because we believe (correctly or not) that we have a better chance to survive in a hospital.

The modern hospital is a place where doctors and patients meet for medical treatment which, it is hoped, will be better than that which could be provided at home. The doctor has two advantages at the hospital: modern technology and expert nursing care. These advantages exist only for the benefit of the patient, but sometimes have the unintended consequence of making the doctor feel more important than he really is. The doctor is no wiser or kinder than he was at home, but he is more confident because he now has people and machines to help him. The patient is happy to see how confident the doctor is, but he feels at a disadvantage because he is now on the doctor's territory. Or is he?

There is a sense in which the hospital is the doctor's territory. Hospitals are built *for* doctors by past, present, and future patients. However, in another sense the doctor is as much a guest in the hospital as the patient. Hospitals are not run by doctors, but by nurses and professional administrators. At the policy-making level there sits not a doctor, or even a group of doctors, but a board of trustees, a board of health, or a university faculty. Even doctors who own their own hospitals usually hire professional administrators. Within the hospital doctors do not have the structural authority—except over their own interns and residents—nurses do. Therein lies the patient's opportunity to protect himself from the doctor's swollen Aesculapian authority. If the patient is a good patient in the eyes of the nurses—which means he demonstrates he is serious about getting well— then he has gained some important leverage with the doctors. It would be a foolish doctor, indeed, who would pit himself against determined nurses.

In one English hospital, a thoracic surgeon began to threaten, nag, and bully a girl who was having a thoracoplasty (the removal of ribs under local anesthetic to collapse the chest wall and rest the tubercular lung). The patient was frightened and began to weep and retch when the surgeon began to crack her ribs with his bone-breaking forceps. The surgeon swore that if she continued to behave so badly he would send her back to the ward and leave her there to die. The nurses did not approve of the surgeon's brutal ways, and went to their matron (nursing director). They said they would no longer work with the surgeon unless he mended his ways. The matron listened to her nurses and told them she would back them to the hilt. The matron demanded that the surgeon apologize to the nurses and to the patient. Although a difficult man, the surgeon was not stupid and recognized a brick wall when he saw one. He apologized.

Florence Nightingale invented the new profession for women* during the Crimean War and thus made the modern hospital possible. When she arrived at the Barrack Hospital in Scutari, Turkey, with her little band of hand-picked nurses, the doctors decided to freeze her out. She instructed her nurses that they were not to tend a single patient until the doctors officially invited them to do so. For a week, the nurses kept to their quarters while the wounded shrieked and died in the wards. But then so many wounded began to pour into the hospital that the doctors could not cope, and Miss Nightingale and her nurses were officially asked to take up their new role. Miss Nightingale understood very clearly the difference between the role of doctor and the role of nurse, and she knew it would be fatal to confuse them and to present nursing as a rival profession to doctoring. She waited for the doctors to see that in order to do their work, they needed something in addition to what their own role provided.

What Miss Nightingale provided was not only bedside nursing, for which she is justly famous, but the sound administration of the hospital based on structural authority. Aesculapian authority mixes poorly with structural authority, but not so nursing. Miss Nightingale *ran* the hospital at Scutari. She provided beds, linens, medicines, bandages, food, lamps, stoves, and, later, writing paper, books, and games for the recovering soldiers. She even provided a French chef, Alexis Soyer, who made delicious meals out of army rations and invented a teapot which could make tea for fifty men and keep it hot. She stated that the first principle of a hospital

---

* The doctor-nurse roles were set up along sex lines, but there is no reason why they must remain so. In *Cancer Ward*, where most of the doctors are female, it seems to make no difference to the role.

was to do the sick no harm, and in order to implement that principle, she set up the administration of the hospital to meet the basic human needs of the patients.

It is still the nurse who provides the basic human comforts, the basic bedside care. Doctors make terrible nurses, and if you wait for your doctor to adjust your pillows more comfortably or to give you a sponge bath, you will have a long wait indeed. One cancer patient found that each of her nurses had a different area of expertise. When the built-in suction machine which came with the room did not work, one nurse commandeered a working older model ("I just tell them that I need two, and then they have to give me one of the old ones"). Another nurse was a genius at creating comfortable bandages out of some wonderful soft, spongy material ("Now I am going to give you a good night's sleep!"). Another discovered that a loudspeaker was just outside the patient's room; she taped a piece of cardboard over it to cut the noise. Others chatted with her, joked with her, and kept up her morale in a thousand little ways. Having never been in a hospital before, this patient was astounded to learn what a large part nurses played in her care and recovery.

People who have never been seriously ill and have never been hospitalized must learn the two roles at the same time, the sick role and that of the hospitalized patient. Stephan Lesher, whose "coronary event" plunged him suddenly into both roles, was a poor student of this curriculum. In their jointly written book, his doctor, Michael Halberstam, reports wearily, "The reactions of the nurses were one sure indication that Lesher was not going to be one of those patients who sail through a coronary and the hospital, leaving only the slightest ripples in their wake." Lesher's motto, according to Halberstam, was that anything worth doing was worth overdoing. Lesher horrified the nurses by doing push-ups two days after his heart attack; he defied them by using the hall bathroom instead of the bedpan or commode. He upset them with his domestic situation, which required that they keep visits from his wife and his new lover from overlapping.

Dr. Halberstam had no doubts that antagonizing the nurses was a very poor idea. "Your doctor visits you perhaps fifteen or twenty minutes a day. The nurses are there all the time. If you get them angry, watch out!" He also notes that nurses, unlike interns, residents, or attending physicians, have a formal changing of the guard. When a new shift takes over, the nurses review each patient. If a patient is acting badly, the news will be passed from one shift to the next. Says Halberstam, "Rules aren't for doctors; they are for nurses. And patients. And a patient who breaks the rules, who offends against the written and unwritten code as Lesher had done, may be in for a hospitalization that seems a good deal longer than it really is."

The nurses soon learned of Lesher's plan to separate from his wife and they disapproved. One nurse explained by saying nurses were middle-class. But perhaps there was a more important reason for their disapproval: Lesher seemed to be giving a good deal more energy to fending off visits from his wife and arranging visits with his new lover than in fighting his illness. It was not middle-class morality but medical morality that was offended. If you are not going to devote yourself to fighting for your life, what are you doing taking up space in a hospital bed? If you want the cooperation of the nurses in battling for your survival, you had better make it clear that you are serious about being a patient.

No doubt some of Lesher's bad behavior was a response to his terror at being in a hospital for the first time, with a heart attack. It is difficult to sort out the fears brought about by hospitalization from those the illness brings. The sorting out of these two fears was expressed in the dream of a patient which he calls "My Next Operation." Sheldon Kopp, a psychotherapist, had brain surgery to remove a tumor which proved benign. However, it was not possible to remove the tumor entirely, and so he was faced with the possibility of enduring the same operation again. He dreamed what this would be like.

In his dream, as he relates in *If You Meet the Buddha on the Road, Kill Him!*, he finds that, this time, the hospital and its routines are familiar to him. "This time I knew which plane to take to Boston, where to find a taxi to take me to the hospital, even which entrance to use. A whirl of familiar impressions followed, of administrative procedures as I signed in, was given a room, and underwent preliminary preparations and diagnostic tests. I knew them all. I'd been through it all before."

Then, he greets the doctors and nurses by name, recognizing them all. He is pleased to find that his favorite doctor, a Chinese neurosurgeon, is to perform the operation. He goes on to say, "And then it happened. Just as he placed the mask over my face, all at once I knew. The bad trip was to begin again. Again it would be a time of terror. I suddenly understood that though I knew how to get to the hospital, understood the procedures I was to undergo, recognized everyone on the staff, and even felt close to my Chinese surgeon, all of this would change nothing. The knowing would not help. I would awaken again psychotic, bewildered, terrified, and in the horror of pain, with my future hanging in uncertain balance."

The patient's first priority in the hospital is to survive—not to be comfortable. But being comfortable certainly helps! One of the most effective ways of having a more comfortable or, at least, less uncomfortable hospitalization is to master a few simple pain-control techniques. The daily routine in any modern hospital involves a good deal of pain. Blood is drawn at least once a day, sometimes more, and many diagnostic tests and medical treatments are painful. Natural stoics are hard to find, but anyone can learn relaxation methods. One woman used the various breathing techniques she had learned in her natural childbirth classes some years before.

She found that shallow mouth breathing with a slack jaw controlled the pain of any procedure that allowed her to be on her back, but she had to use deep breathing to get through some procedures, such as a spinal tap and a bone marrow test, which required that she lie on her side. Doctors and nurses are pleasantly surprised when a patient demonstrates some mastery over pain—so surprised that it can't happen very often. Perhaps it would be easier on everyone concerned if a bit of nursing time were devoted to teaching new patients some relaxation skills.

Even the simplest comforts are hard to come by in the hospital. Silence, for example. One man, a musician with a well-trained ear, found that listening to fourteen hours of uninterrupted canned music—cocktail-hour music, as he called it—a day was a form of torture, especially since the cocktails, which alone would have made it bearable, were not forthcoming. He asked the nurses about it, and they said that they hated it, too; it greatly added to the stress of their day. It seemed that no one in the hospital could control either the volume or the duration of these unwanted concerts. The music was piped in directly from the company that purveyed it and had sold it to the hospital—for the good of the patients, of course. The patient began to wonder whether he might rather grapple with his illness at home, dying, perhaps, to Bach and Beethoven, or Simon and Garfunkel, rather than living while listening to "Tea for Two" for the four-hundredth time. But the will to survive prevailed and he endured his stay. However, should he require hospitalization again, he plans to inquire whether he is likely to become a captive audience again. The hospital had no right to impose this noise pollution on its patients. Nothing in the medical literature suggests patients recover better when subjected to music over which they have no control, and no one had asked either the patients or the nurses how they felt about it.

In a general way, the hospital is set up to ensure the survival of patients. But for each patient, the illness and the hospitalization are unique experiences. Only the patient knows the particulars of what his body and his soul need in order to survive and flourish. Here we must follow Dr. William Nolen's principle, as stated in *Surgeon Under the Knife*, that no one cares for the patient as much as the patient cares for himself. The musician-patient did not know that once he survived the operation itself, his worst torment would be canned music, but now he does know, and so it is up to him to see that it does not happen again.

Lesher did not know he would need so much information, so much reassurance, so much repetition of the facts of his case. Dr. Halberstam had no way of knowing what this particular patient would need from his doctor and from the hospital staff. All he could know is that every patient is different. Halberstam writes, "I think Lesher's illness has changed my approach to other coronary patients a bit. I'm more explicit in outlining the possible mood changes they may go through. I'm a bit more detailed and dogmatic for those patients who need the reassurance of a written schedule. I've tried to be more tolerant of patients who need the same information repeated over and over again." There is, Halberstam notes, "an enormous difference between doctoring and patienting." Halberstam and Lesher were no more able to abolish that difference than any other doctor-patient pair, but they did learn to listen to each other.

Sometimes going into the hospital proves to be a mistake and then one's best move is to get out. A woman who had advanced multiple sclerosis and lived alone allowed well-meaning neighbors to take her into the hospital. She soon made the decision that there was little the hospital could do for her, although the doctors urged her to stay. She preferred to endure her illness at home, and so she called a cab and left. We are sometimes prisoners of our illness but we need not be prisoners of the hospital.

We enter a hospital in order to save our lives, and the hospital architecture reflects that. The admitting office, the emergency room, the private room or ward, the operating room, the recovery room, the intensive care unit are all architectural expressions of some aspect of our treatment and care. But what if we are dying? There is no space in the hospital which reflects the needs of the dying, no room that is comparable in its function to those set up for the sick role.* The patient, the family, and the staff may all know the patient is dying, yet the sick-role architecture makes it difficult to express this.

If you are dying, what are your spatial options? You may go home, if there is someone to care for you. You may go to a hospice, a nursing home, or some equivalent. Or you may stay at the hospital. If you stay at the hospital and are alert enough to make your own decisions (which will otherwise be made by your family or, failing that, by the staff) you will want to make it absolutely clear you have moved out of the sick role and into the dying role.† That gives you the right to refuse medical treatments which can no longer help you, tests which will no longer tell you anything, and restrictions of diet, of pain-killers, or of visitors which no longer make sense. You can gratefully accept the efforts of the doctors and nurses to make you comfortable—for now comfort of every sort *is* your highest priority . . . including spiritual comfort. You may want visits from spiritual advisors or simply from people you cherish with whom you can communicate freely about this ultimate human situation. The center of the affair is now not the doctor, the nurse, or the patient—for there is no more patient—but the dying person.‡

For the patient in the hospital, the most illuminating question is "What am I doing here?" Whether you are having diagnostic tests, getting a medical treatment, or undergoing a

---

*The morgue doesn't count—the patient is (one hopes) dead before he gets there.

† For a fuller discussion of the dying role, see Chapter XV.

‡We do not seem to have a name for a person who occupies the dying role.

surgical procedure, your purpose ought to be to improve or safeguard your health or your life. That purpose will be the source of your strength in enduring what must be endured. If you have no such purpose, but have found yourself in the hospital because your doctor told you to come there, or your family brought you, or you were frightened, then you may feel like a prisoner and perhaps behave like one. And that will certainly not bring out the best in the doctors and nurses who care for you.

In a very real sense, we, as patients and potential patients, *own* the hospitals. We pay for them through our medical fees, our insurance, our taxes, our churches, our community efforts. Many of us would refuse to move to a place which did not have a modern hospital. Yet when we enter a hospital, we often feel like the guests of some giant in a fairy story— we are not quite sure whether we have been invited for dinner or whether we *are* the dinner. We may be truly powerless over our illnesses and, certainly, over our mortality, but we can alter the degree of powerlessness we feel over the hospital by learning to be responsible patients and so eliciting the best possible response from the doctors and nurses we have caused to be there. The hospital is our territory, too.

VIII *Patients in the Family*

ILLNESS STRIKES FAMILIES; what determines how well the family can strike back? Families that have been through many illnesses know how to size up a new one and how to man their battle stations until it is over. Those which have lead a disease-free life, either because of genetic endowment, preventive measures, or good luck, have the smallest fund of useful knowledge on how to cope with illness. But even these families often display unexpected resourcefulness.

Families must know when to confer the sick role; that's crucial. Family members know, better than anyone, what the sick person is like: how he looks, what he eats, how much sleep he gets, whether he is cheerful or taciturn. What alerts the family to the possibility of illness is a change, especially an unexplained change, in normal habits. Ellen Levit's mother noticed that Ellen was eating less and getting thinner. Later, she berated herself for accepting Ellen's explanation of teenage dieting; in fact, cancer had caused Ellen to lose her appetite.

Very often the first sign of illness the family notices is a change in affect: the patient-to-be becomes grumpy, sullen, irritable, seclusive, sarcastic, or ill-tempered. The ill person may believe he is signaling illness when all he is signaling is bad feeling. The family, who are the victims of this error in signaling, quite naturally get angry. The home atmosphere becomes so strained that even the belated recognition of illness will not set it straight.

The sick role is not accorded because of bad feeling, but only because of illness. Part of the function of the sick role is to filter out the bad feelings which would otherwise obscure what needs to be done to combat the illness. Elation, flippancy, depression, anguish, despair, resentment, and suspicion are all "noise" in the system. One of the reasons that depressive illnesses so often fail to command the sick role is because they release so much affect in both the ill person and those around him that the illness itself is frequently missed.

The wise family member, then, is alert to the possibility of illness when another family member shows bad affect for no apparent reason. One might call this the first degree of alertness: someone might be sick. Often the situation resolves itself: the bad affect is about some real-life problem or just a bad mood, or it is an illness but a trivial one which heals on its own?

The second degree of alertness is: someone is sick, but it's not serious. Most illnesses are not serious, and what may be needed is simply tender loving care. A minor illness may even be a happy oasis in family life—a little more time for a husband and wife to spend together, a new coloring book for a small child, a tray of special treats for a sick teenager. Some people believe that time spent sick should be as unpleasant as possible to discourage future attempts, but Paul Berkman, in an article which appeared in *Medical Care*, found that there appeared to be survival value in spending a modest amount of time per year in the sick role:

Taking survival as a criterion of health, it would appear that a modicum of yearly indulgence in the sick role is healthier than none at all. Presupposing that almost everyone experiences some below-par or "sniffle" days throughout the year . . . the Sick-Indoors findings suggest that in the long run (i.e., for survival) it is better to acknowledge the fact and to spend a few of them admittedly sick and restricted in activity, rather than to ignore (or deny) them entirely in favor of the everyday routine. Further, the Sick-Abed findings similarly indicate that with sickness thus acknowledged, it is still better to spend some of the days in bed most of the time.

With children, minor illnesses provide an opportunity to teach proper sick-role behavior which may be needed later on. An illness, like a story, has a beginning, a middle, and an end. The mother places the child in the sick role in response to his complaints or her own observations. The child's usual activities are curtailed: he will not go to school, he will stay in his pajamas instead of getting dressed, his mother will take his temperature, etc. These changes in his usual life show the child that being in the sick role has consequences. If the child is not sick but has said he is, and his mother has taken him at his word, he then learns that "being sick" is different from being home on a weekend or a holiday. He may find that the duties of the sick role outweigh its rights. However, if the child *is* sick, he finds his mother is willing to take that seriously and to care for him so that he gets well and is as comfortable as possible till then. The child finds the sick role is well worth having *if he is sick*. As the child gets better, the balance tips in the other direction: staying in bed is now a constriction of his activities, and he signals this by being annoyed rather than grateful for his mother's attentions. The experienced mother notices this shift and says: "Perhaps you could have your breakfast at the table this morning." The child relinquishes the rights and duties of the sick role, resumes his usual rights and duties, and normalcy is restored. The child has learned a valuable lesson about that sequence of events we call illness.

Mothers learn to make very fine judgments about whether a child is ill and, if so, how ill. A mother may decide that a child is not as ill as he claims and so she insists he go to school. Later, the school nurse may call and say: "Mrs. X., we have Jimmy here in our office. He has a temperature of 103. Can you come and get him?" The mother now feels guilty about having sent a sick child to school; she feels embarrassed at being thought an unobservant or harsh mother. The next time she will take a closer look at her child before making a decision. A mother who makes the opposite mistake and keeps a child home when he is not really sick will find herself with a bored, restless child who wants to know why he has no one to play with. The next time she will think twice before conferring the sick role.

Sometimes a child claims to be sick and wants to stay home from school; this child has a psychological problem at school: another child who bullies or a teacher who is too demanding. Then the mother can use the child's day at home to find out what the real problem is and what can be done about it. But what kind of note does the mother write the next day: "Johnny was sick yesterday" or "Johnny stayed home because he was afraid that Bobby was going to beat him up?" That depends on the mother's assessment of the teacher's understanding and on the child's preferences. A child may prefer to handle his problems privately without involving the teacher or he may prefer to get his teacher's support.

There are also problems of temperament. One mother had a child who did well in school and had many friends, but found the daily routine of going to school very burdensome. This little girl was exceptionally imaginative and seemed to need quite a bit of time alone to enjoy her own imagination. Many mothers would have said: "Nonsense! She has to learn to live with routines." But this mother was concerned that the child might get progressively more turned off to school, and her long-range goal was to have the child get as much education as her intelligence warranted. She was also afraid she would force her daughter to pretend to be sick if that was the only way the child could get the days at home she apparently needed. So the mother decided on a trade-off: the child could stay home as many days as she thought would not cause problems at school; the mother agreed to write notes saying that the child was "sick" on those days. In return, the child would *never* say she was sick when she was not. In this way, the child's sick-role behavior was kept intact. One day that turned out to be very important, for as the mother was going off to work, the child said she was sick and the mother believed her. Within hours, the child was on the operating table, getting life-saving surgery. Had the child herself been confused about whether or not she was sick, or had the mother come to believe the child often lied about being sick, this urgent illness might have been ignored and the child might have died.

Being a sick housewife is a special problem. The wife and mother is usually the person who confers the sick role on other members of the family in minor illnesses. Typically, it is she who takes care of the household patients. When she becomes ill she must confer the sick role on herself, something she may have done readily before she was married. As a housewife she doesn't earn "sick leave," and since she works at home, she appears to be "on duty" as long as the other members of the family can see her. She is likely to feel guilty about being sick because of the highly personal nature of her relationship with her "employers." Often, an unhappy compromise is reached: she totters around grumpily, doing her usual duties, while letting her family know she feels awful. The best thing to do would be to firmly announce "I am sick" and disappear from sight into the bedroom, renouncing responsibility for running the house until the illness has receded. This will do less damage in the long run than carrying on in a bad temper. The fact that she carries the role of homemaker does not mean that the other family members are literally incapable for feeding and dressing themselves.

What happens when the homemaker cannot get the sick role? If a woman has no right to be sick, but is too ill to function, she may have to assume the impaired role,* "take to bed," and lower her family's expectations of her altogether, which may have been the reason for many a Victorian invalid. Among the rights women today are demanding, none is more crucial than equal access to the sick role. The doctor who says his female patient is "just a neurotic housewife" instead of investigating her actual symptoms is denying her the sick role on a sexist basis and forcing her into the lower-status impaired role. Women with full-time careers often do no better in getting the sick role: they are told they feel unwell because they are denying their femininity by taking their work seriously. Those with a full-time job *and* a homemaker job are told they feel sick because they are doing too much! It's hard to win with a sexist doctor, but the sick role is a fundamental, inalienable human right and should be fought for.

Now we come to the third degree of alertness: someone is sick, and it's serious. Once this determination is made, families are capable of the most extraordinary exertions on behalf of their sick member. *Son-Rise,* a book by Barry Kaufman, tells of a remarkable family effort to save a child suffering from Kanner's syndrome, or early infantile autism. This apparently normal child, Raun, displayed only one unusual behavior during his first year: he did not put out his arms to be picked up. Otherwise, he was smiling, laughing, and playing like any other one-year-old. After the first year, Raun began to hear more and more inconsistently, as if he were intermittently deaf. By the time Raun was seventeen months old, the

---

*For a fuller discussion of the impaired role, see chapter XIII.

Kaufmans, who seem to be an exceptionally alert and sensitive family, realized something was very wrong. Raun was now hypnotically fascinated with inanimate objects, he had developed a repetitious motion of his fingers against his lips, he looked through other people as if they were transparent, and he was not developing any language. The Kaufmans made a rapid and thorough search of the literature on childrens' disorders and found Leo Kanner's article, written in 1943, defining the condition of early infantile autism. The description fit Raun's symptoms. They found that the literature on autism was extremely pessimistic about prognosis, and when the made the rounds of professional people who had treated this condition, they found further cause for gloom. They wrote, "We felt we had to intervene and do it now. Each day we could see him slipping from us, withdrawing. Becoming more encapsulated. Raun seemed bewildered too. Medical and institutional help was not available."

The Kaufmans had a philosophy, a theory, and a technique. The philosophy was called Option Method, and its basic premise was "to love is to be happy with." They decided to enjoy Raun day by day and not to regard their situation as tragic. Their theory was that autism was something like a stroke in that a portion of the brain was damaged, but other parts of the brain could be trained to take over the necessary functions. Their technique was sensory stimulation in a non-threatening environment. They developed a program calling for seventy-five hours a week of input and exposure. They did not question his "isms," as they called his repetitious behaviors, but when he rocked, they rocked with him, and when he spun plates, they all spun plates. Objects are predictable to a damaged brain, but people are not, so they did their best to make themselves more predictable. They worked with him in the bathroom, because it was the smallest, simplest, and least-confusing room in the house. They fed him always at eye level, using his need for food as a way of increasing eye contact with him. In order to put in the many hours of training they felt Raun needed, they brought in young volunteers to help them. After eight weeks of the new program, Raun cried to get something. Later, they decided they would no longer give Raun things when he cried for them—they "played dumb" and pretended they did not know what he wanted. They wanted him to say the word for what he wanted and were rewarded one day when Raun asked for "wa" (water).

Whenever Raun was physically ill, even slightly, he returned to his old ritualized behaviors. Then they had to hold on to their philosophy that their love for him was not conditional on his improvement. Once, after nine days of regression, Raun "returned" to them and to his newer ways of behaving. They wondered what this meant: was he comparing the old and the new? At two years, after thirty weeks of their intensive program, Raun tested at the twenty-four-month level in half the tests; in the other half, at the thirty-month level. In *You Are Not Alone,* Clara Park, an expert on autism, says of him, "The earliest intervention (17 months) and the most hopeful outcome yet reported."

If a family can defeat such a devastating illness on their own, why does one need doctors? Our celebration of the Kaufmans' splendid work should in no way deceive us about the part played by professional people in Raun's improvement. Barry Kaufman was able to search the literature because there was a literature to be searched. Because Leo Kanner described and named the syndrome he observed clinically, other doctors, psychologists, and educators were able to recognize the same syndrome when they saw it. Slowly a body of knowledge accumulated about this syndrome, telling of many efforts, most of them not very successful, to treat it. What the Kaufmans found was a diagnosis and a prognosis, plus a run-down of what had or had not worked with this condition. They saved a great deal of precious time by focusing their efforts so precisely. They could not have done this if they had had to start from scratch. They would not have done as well even ten years earlier.

Sometimes what a family must supply to its seriously ill member is discipline and the courage to go on. The Massies had confronted hundreds of crises in the course of living with Bobby's hemophilia, but one day they found they were up against something new. Faced with another episode of internal bleeding with its excruciating pain, Bobby refused to have his leg put in a cast. His morale had snapped. "Unhinged with pain, Bobby was at last showing all the horror he had felt, encased in plaster, during his young years. He had borne it so valiantly, with such strength. He had not complained. Perhaps he hadn't known how. But the suffering and constraint of those years were making his present pain sharper, his agony more intense." Suzanne Massie tried all the tricks she knew to get her son through the endless nights of pain, but this time they did not work. Then, in the middle of the third night, she realized something had to be done: either Bobby conquered the pain or the pain would conquer him. She told him that she was going to get him up and into the living room. Then she made her son tell her about the moon flight. He said, "I can't. I can't." But she insisted, and at last he told her about the events of the moon shot. This forced recital broke the hold the pain had over him; she wheeled him back to his bed and, for the first time in three days, he fell asleep. In *Journey*, she wrote, "He slept only an hour and then woke in pain again. But the pain was no longer an omnipotent fiend but only our old familiar enemy which would, with patience, recede like a terrible tide."

Illness is never an excuse for bad behavior, and the more serious the illness, the more dangerous it is to allow the sick person to fall into evil ways. Although Suzanne Massie understood full well how awful the pressures were on Bobby, she understood even better that it would be literally fatal to allow him to indulge in self-pity, to refuse medical treatment, or to become dependent on pain-killing drugs. Only the most steely self-discipline could preserve Bobby's life and allow him to attain manhood, and this she was able to offer him.

The families of the mentally ill have more difficulty insisting on good behavior from their sick young people than the Massies. They tend to be uncertain about whether they are dealing with "real" illnesses or whether their children are emotionally damaged. They wobble back and forth between allowing themselves to be tyrannized by their sick family member and making demands which the sick person cannot possibly meet. Their uncertainty generates shame and guilt, and this leads to the isolation of the family from the larger community, which, in turn, cuts them off from the kind of information that would make them less uncertain. In an effort to help families break out of this vicious circle, Clara Park* wrote *You Are Not Alone,* an encyclopedic book of advice for the families of the mentally ill. In the book she instructs families about the many things they can do, indeed, ought to do, to assert their rights and take up their duties: how to find help in the Yellow Pages, what kinds of treatments and therapies are available, how to prepare a medical history, how to request a consultation, what your legal rights are, how to ask for a reasonable fee (take your latest income-tax return and a list of fixed expenses), how to evaluate schools and hospitals, how to organize a consumer group.

Reasonably enough, Clara Park suggests that the more a family understands its expectations, the less frustrated and disappointed they are likely to be. In the chapter "How to Consult a Mental Health Professional," she asks, "What do you—and your relative—expect from this consultation? Encouraging support? Deep exploration? Practical help? A thorough assessment of physical factors and treatment according to the medical model?" The same questions might be asked

---

*Herself the mother of a Kanner's syndrome child and the author of *The Siege,* a classic account of this condition.

where the illness is physical: what do you expect the doctor
to do for you? It might be worthwhile to write out a list of expectations for *all* the participants involved: what do you expect of the sick person? Do you expect him to be well in two
weeks? Two years? Do you expect him to be living with you
when he's forty? Do you expect him to keep track of his own
medication? Do you expect him to be cheerful? Do you expect
him to eat at the table with the rest of the family? What do
you expect of yourself? Do you expect to suspend all your activities until the sick member of your family gets well? Or do
you expect to carry on as if nothing had happened? Do you
expect to have to learn a great deal about the illness? What do
you expect of the doctor? That he will tell you everything you
need to know about the illness? That he will let you know if
things take a turn for the worst? That he will call in other
doctors if he is stumped? By making the expectations of all
the participants explicit you can find out whether they are
founded on reality, whether they are based on mistaken information, whether the other participants agree about them,
and whether you are asking too much or too little of the sick
person, the family, and the professionals involved.

If a family is in for a long siege with a difficult illness, they
would do well to contact some other families that have lived
with the illness longer. This can be done through a public organization devoted to the particular illness or perhaps your
medical specialist can suggest how to contact other families
like your own. Why try to figure out everything for yourself
when someone else has already been there?

Fortunately, today's families are letting us know how they
cope with serious illness by writing books about it. We now
have accounts of families coping with cancer, leukemia, hemophilia, stroke, schizophrenia, retardation, autism, brain
damage, deafness, and no doubt there will be books about
other illnesses. They are not fun to read, and one can only
wish that the events they record had never happened. But

they are a better way for families to learn about illness than the previous method: by losing most of their children.

Not all families are called upon to put forth the heroic efforts recorded in accounts like those of the Kaufmans or the Massies. Fortunately, most families are required to do much less and can hold to a simpler standard of responsible patienthood behavior. The family must recognize when one of their members is ill; refrain from blaming themselves, the ill person, or anyone else; seek the best available medical help and cooperate with that help; nurse their patient back to health (or help him to depart in peace); and learn what they can about avoiding illnesses or preventing their recurrence. These skills need to be passed along from generation to generation, and families have been doing just that for a very long time.

IX *Patients Convalescing*

CONVALESCENCE, LIKE MOURNING, is a lost art. Those of us who have no experience with illness quite naturally have no idea how to convalesce. Stephan Lesher, when he was in the hospital, frantically besieged his doctor for instructions about what he would or would not be able to do when he went home. Dr. Halberstam was at first annoyed with his patient's insistent demands for a detailed schedule and thought it sufficient to give some general instructions about "taking it easy." But Lesher's idea of taking it easy was to start reporting the Watergate scandal, and he was soon back in the hospital with chest pains. Two bouts of pleurisy later, Dr. Halberstam conceded that some patients need very specific instructions if they are to stay well.

In the old days, things were different. Many more people died untimely deaths, but those who survived an illness looked forward to a long and carefully paced convalescence. This was to prevent relapses which might prove as dangerous as the original illness. Very little could be done medically for most patients and so a great deal of attention had to be paid to stimulating the patient's natural restorative powers.

The doctor in Samuel Butler's *The Way of All Flesh* gives the most meticulous instructions for Ernest Pontifex, recovering from "brain fever" and a host of personal catastrophes. He says, "I have found the Zoological Gardens of service to many of my patients. I should prescribe for Mr. Pontifex a course of the larger mammals. Don't let him think he is taking them medicinally, but let him go to their house twice a week for a fortnight, and stay with the hippopotamus, the rhinoceros, and the elephants, till they begin to bore him. I find these beasts do my patients more good than any others. The monkeys . . . do not stimulate sufficiently. The larger carnivora are unsympathetic. The reptiles are worse than useless, and the marsupials are not much better. . . ." The doctor then goes on to give a list of other inexpensive and available activities which will contribute to his patient's recovery.

Convalescence is a time for indulgence; the illness has abated, the treatments have had their effects, and now body and soul must heal. Indulgence acts as a reward for having conquered the illness and a lure to entice the once-sick person back into a state of good health. Here the convalescent role differs from the sick role, for the sick person must forgo not only indulgences, but even the most ordinary comforts in the service of getting well. It isn't until after the illness has subsided or the operation is over that the traditional gifts of fresh flowers, fruit, and candy arrive for the convalescent. Now is the time to be good to oneself.

Laura Bohannan, in *Return to Laughter*, describes how she moves from the sick role to the convalescent role as she recovers from a fever:

Then I was better, well enough to lie in my deck chair and do nothing. I wanted only dark and quiet. Tears of weak irritation ran down my cheeks because I could not shut out the bleating of kids and goats, the rustle and flutter of chickens on my thatch, the squalling of babies, the swish of grindstones, thump of mortars, shouted conversations and the constant drumming. Sounds that I usually managed to relegate to the background, noticing them no more than the hiss of my lamp at night, now tormented me. I could think of nothing more beautiful than the black-and-white sign at home, HOSPITAL STREET. QUIET.

I only wanted to be let alone. I could not bear the jostle of people. Their life was too strong for me; it hurt me as the light hurt my eyes.

Then she luckily discovered some detective stories that she had hidden away for just such an emergency:

By the end of the three-day rain-granted peace and the five detective stories, in only one of which I was able to guess the murderer, I had almost completely recovered. The next morning was fresh and blue; the soaked thatch popped and rustled cheerfully as it dried in the sun. I was gay with the clear morning air and that first wonderful moment of recovery when one's body feels as good and wholesome as newly baked bread. The people by whom I had felt persecuted were today familiar faces and old acquaintances; conversation with them, which had seemed so impossible, the most natural and pleasant thing in the world.

Not everyone allows himself the pleasure of reading detective stories and hiding from the demands of others. One woman, recovering from a long illness, accepted the invitation of some friends to convalesce in their home. The day of her arrival, and the next day, she basked in the wonderful experience of being cared for and having no responsibilities. But by the third day she felt guilty that she was not working on some papers she had brought with her. She spent one miserable day in a role-less limbo, neither well enough to work nor sick enough to ask for help but somewhere in-between—convalescent. She had never convalesced from any illness before, and so she had no idea how to behave. Her hosts, who were both medical people, gently instructed her, and so she settled down to read a book about—shades of Samuel Butler!—elephants! Very gradually, she began to help

out a bit in the house and to work a bit on her papers until
the convalescent period seemed to melt away of its own and
quite suddenly she knew it was over and made plans to return to her own home.

Some people do not find convalescence to their taste; it is a
great come-down from the drama of illness. Charles Lamb,
writing as "Elia," was one of those who enjoyed too much of
what is now called the "secondary gains" of illness. In *Last
Essays of Elia* he moaned, "How convalescence shrinks a man
back to his pristine stature! where now is the space which he
occupied so lately, in his own, the family's eye?" Yet he
knew well enough that he could not linger indefinitely in the
sickroom, "In this flat swamp of convalescence, left by the
ebb of sickness, yet far enough from the terra firma of established health, your note, dear Editor, reached me request-
ing—an article. . . . The summons, unseasonable as it appeared, seemed to link me again to the petty business of life,
however trivial; a wholesome meaning from that prepos-
terous dream of self-absorption—the puffy state of sickness—
in which I confess to have lain so long."

Charles Lamb had difficulty taking up his life again after
an illness which lasted "some weeks." But it is quite another
matter to take up one's life again after some years of being ill.
If the illness lasts so short a time that it does not disrupt
one's social existence, then it almost does not matter how ill
one has been. But if the illness lasts long enough—say, over a
year—then the social fabric of one's life may be so torn that
one despairs of ever patching it together again. This is the
story Jessamyn West tells of her illness and her mother's efforts to seduce her back into life in *The Woman Said Yes: Encounters with Life and Death.*

Jessamyn West developed tuberculosis while a graduate
student. When she first learned her diagnosis, she was jubi-
lant: she had a real illness, she was not crazy, not a malingerer. But her joy was short-lived, because she soon found
herself living in a "san" (sanatorium) with her fellow pa-

tients dying all around her. At first she believed, as so many patients do, that if she followed every rule she would get well. But the "san" was not graduate school, and after two years, the doctors advised her mother to take her home to die among her loved ones.

Jessamyn's mother, Grace, knew nothing about tuberculosis, but she knew a lot about life. A naturally disorderly person, she began to infuse Jessamyn's feeble existence with her own strong sense of living. "Why don't you turn on your radio?" she asked. "I couldn't. The radio brought me the world outside my room. I didn't want to think of it, to be tormented with reports of people who had lives to live; who went to work, attended seminars, played tennis, swam at the beaches, bought food at the grocery store." But Grace was insistent, "Turn on your radio for one minute. . . . One minute only, and then you can turn it off." Jessamyn did, and heard Bing Crosby singing "Wagon Wheels," and it "opened a small-sized door for me into the world I had lost."

Jessamyn could not live in the past, which she had lost; she had no present, and could not envision a future. So her mother made her a gift of *her* past. Too weak even to read, Jessamyn was able to listen to her mother's stories of Quaker life in southern Indiana at the turn of the century. In the journal where she had been writing down her temperature and weight, Jessamyn began to record the dialect of her mother's people.

A friend brought Jessamyn a kitten named Samantha. Grace disliked cats, but she knew a healer when she saw one. Jessamyn still could not stand or walk or read, but she could caress and touch. She had never had a pet, there had never been time, but now she began to care for her kitten. Her doctor said, "You began to get well the day that cat arrived."

Jessamyn got well enough to return to her husband and her own home, but she still lived the life of an invalid. The one form of life she permitted herself was to sit propped up in bed and write the stories her mother had told her.

These stories were finally published in a book, *The Friendly Persuasion*.

When the book came out, Jessamyn was invited to New York for two weeks as the guest of the publisher. The prospect terrified her. "I would faint at an interview, collapse at a cocktail party, die face to face with a live editor," she told her mother. Grace said, "You are already dead, living as you do. Afraid to take a deep breath, or laugh till you cry, or cry till you run out of tears." Should I go, then, Jessamyn asked. "I think you are starting another kind of sickness if you don't. Worse than the other. In the mind, not the body." And so she went, a writer among writers, and had the time of her life.

Some people are ill so long that in addition to the usual problems of convalescence, they have to adapt to a world that has changed since they became ill. One young man, who had had a severe schizophrenic illness, reemerged into an increasingly normal life in the late 1960s. He had grown up on a quiet street near Harvard Square, and, except for brief hospitalizations, had lived there with his parents all his life. During the height of his illness, Harvard Square underwent a social revolution. In addition to the absentminded Harvard professors and earnest students, the Square was now hopping with long-haired and bare-footed young people in various altered states of consciousness, members of the Hare Krishna and other sects, street musicians, and all manner of oddly dressed and strangely behaved people. At first, this young man was so pleased to be feeling better that he did not notice the sedate neighborhood of his childhood had changed beyond all recognition. When he did notice, he was deeply shocked. "Did you see how those people were dressed?" he would ask, in a horrified tone. But little by little, he grew accustomed to the lively scene, and after a while, he quietly moved out of his parents' house into his own apartment.

Not all such Rip Van Winkles can adapt, nor can all Sleeping Beauties be awakened. Dr. Oliver Sacks, in working with patients ill for decades with post-encephalitic Parkinson's disease, or sleeping sickness, found a tremendous variation in response to being awakened by the new drug, L-Dopa. In *Awakenings* he tells the story of one woman, whom he calls Rose R., who had been afflicted in 1926. When she was awakened in 1969, she responded briefly and dramatically, singing songs and talking in a lively way about the events of her twenty-first year. She was thrilled at first to be liberated from her Parkinsonian prison, but could not comprehend or tolerate the reality of her situation, that she was sixty-four years old and that it was 1969. The drug ceased to work for her, and she returned, for the most part, to her earlier zombie-like state.

Also in *Awakenings,* Dr. Sacks tells of another Parkinsonian patient, Mrs. T., who had lain rigid, mute, and motionless for *forty-eight years!* When Dr. Sacks first saw her, she weighed four hundred pounds and lay on a specially reinforced bed. She was evidently able to reward her nurses from time to time with smiles and kisses, for they were fond of her and gave her devoted care. Since her family was no longer in contact with her, Dr. Sacks took it upon himself to give her L-Dopa—although Mrs. T. had indicated that she didn't want it. The results were so good that she said, "Thank God you had sense to get it inside me!" The rigidity of her great body "cracked," and she began to move and talk in a more normal fashion.

Now what can convalescence mean for a woman "dead" for forty-eight years? At first, she talked and sang songs from her past, in a strong Yiddish-Polish accent. She had indeed awakened, but only to her past. Dr. Sack's problem was to give her some life in the present. He started by buying for her a small cactus plant. She was very pleased with it and watched it for hours. Then she began to form a relationship with the physiotherapist who bathed and massaged her and

designed special implements with which her deformed
hands could hold things. Meanwhile, a social worker was attempting to locate Mrs. T.'s daughter, and after almost three
years, she was successful. The daughter had been told that
her mother was dead—which in a sense was true. After
about a year of understandably difficult visits, Mrs. T. and
her daughter began to enjoy each other's company. Dr. Sacks
says, "One could see, in these intervening months, how Mrs.
T. became humanized from week to week, as she emerged
from her pit of regression, desolation, and unreality. This
one good relation was the thread which led the way from the
maze of madness, which drew her forth from the depths of
Unbeing." Thus a woman convalesced from a catastrophic
illness which had taken forty-eight years of her life but
which had not broken her spirit.

Just as almost anyone can bumble through a short, acute
illness, almost anyone can get through a short convalescence.
Whatever mistakes are made will soon be forgotten along
with the illness. But those who have had illnesses for many
years, even though their stories may not be as dramatic as
that of Mrs. T., can expect a long and tricky convalescence.

The problem is that one adapts to a long illness, molds
one's life around it. A person ill for many years may develop
an erratic pattern of relating to his or her spouse and children. The family members grow accustomed to this and
make their own adaptation to it; therefore they resist change.
This is a well-known phenomenon in the families of alcoholics. The wife who has had to support the family for years
because her husband drank, while enlisting the sympathy of
others for being so unlucky, may be quite confused if her
husband one day stops drinking, starts earning a living, and
begins to discipline the children. It is not unknown for a wife
in such a situation to tempt her newly sober husband with a
drink. The husband, with his new-found sobriety, must then
cope with two problems: the actual changes within himself

which accompany such a radical alteration of habits and his family's resistance to the reemergence of the long-lost husband and father.

The problem is much the same if it is the wife who is the alcoholic. Joyce Rebeta-Burditt, in *The Cracker Factory*, her fictionalized account of a woman's recovery from alcoholism, has her heroine, Cassie, say, "At first Charlie thanked me so fervently for breakfast every morning that I was convinced he'd been awake all night praying for cornflakes and toast. I washed his socks out by hand, gray ones and black ones and brown ones, hung them neatly in rows and tucked them tidily into a corner of his dresser drawer. We were polite, considerate, thoughtful and entirely unnatural." Since Charlie had been making the breakfast and looking after the children and socks for many years, as well as supporting the family, it took a bit of getting used to for all of them to have Cassie sober.

Alcoholics Anonymous talks of a honeymoon period, when a person first stops drinking and realizes he can overcome this devastating illness. This is the same phenomenon described by Laura Bohannan after her illness had passed. Everything looks wonderful and the ordinary joys of life take on psychedelic intensity. But experienced A.A. people know the honeymoon is often followed by a period of depression as the recovering alcoholic soberly assesses the difficulties of taking up his life again. They try to warn their new members that this will happen so the shock of it will not drive them to drink. A.A. people are probably better informed about convalescence than any other group of people who have suffered from a chronic illness. A person recovering from some other long-standing illness who was looking for guidelines could do worse than to attend some A.A. meetings.

The central issue in convalescence is forgiveness. The rule seems to be that unless you can forgive yourself and others for your illness, you cannot recover. Recovery depends on accepting the sick role, which means you do not blame yourself or others for your illness. If you are still blaming yourself for your illness, you will tend to push yourself beyond what you can do at your stage of recovery and will very likely suffer a relapse. If you blame others, you will be tempted to do too little in order to show them how sick you still are and how much they are to blame. What you need to be doing is making an accurate assessment, day by day, of what you can or cannot do at that particular stage of recovery. If you have overshot the mark, you need to pull back as gracefully as possible; if you are doing less than you can, you must endure the anxiety and discomfort of exerting yourself a bit more. The best thing is not to get sick, but if you do, the next best thing is to fully and completely recover. This you cannot do unless you truly forgive yourself. The sick role requires it.

Doctors

X *Doctors as Doctors*

THE SAME AMNESIA WHICH IMPEDES our learning anything
about being ill when we are well also prevents our holding a
steady mental image of the doctor. Sick, we ascribe to him
every power; well, our feelings range from indifference to
envy, suspicion, contempt, indignation, even hatred. The
poet John Owens put it:

> God and the doctor we alike adore,
> But only when in danger, not before;
> The danger o'er, both are alike requited,
> God is forgotten, and the doctor slighted.*

Both God and the doctor are presumably accustomed to our
fickle ways, but however quickly our adoration may fade, we
require a composite picture of the good doctor so that we
may find one again when we need one and encourage the

---

* "Epigrams," in J. R. Whitwell's *Analecta Psychiatrica*.

growth and development of others. Our amnesia also requires that we learn to spot a bad or inappropriate doctor when we see one, for sickness blinds us to the doctor's faults as surely as health blinds us to his virtues.

Essential to our portrait of the exemplary doctor is that he uses his Aesculapian authority for the sole purpose of conferring the sick role in order to benefit the particular, individual patient. In *The Victim Is Always the Same*, I. S. Cooper in making the decision to operate for the first time on a child with dystonia musculorum deformans, spoke of himself thus:

> His criterion for making that decision centered on the individual, the child who had dystonia. His ultimate concern was with her welfare. All of his training, study, preparation had no other meaning at that moment, other than to help that particular child. Did the operation offer her a chance for less pain, for less suffering, a possibility of rehabilitation that could not be found elsewhere? The procedure could not be carried out in an attempt to gain information that might help future children, or in an attempt to learn more about dystonia. If there were secondary gains, so much the better. But the only possible reason for performing that first operation was to alleviate the child's suffering.

The good doctor has to be willing and able to make decisions on the basis of evidence that a scientist would not accept as sufficient; confronted with a patient who needs help, he must act. In *Confessions of a Gynecologist*, an anonymous gynecologist speaks of the loneliness of decision-making in the delivery room:

> Of course there are members of the delivery-room crew all around you, but you, the doctor, have to add up the evidence and make the decision, knowing that a life is at stake. You can't indulge in a leisurely, legalistic weighing of the evidence, pro and con. You're dealing with warm, human flesh, flowing blood, and physical margins that can't be measured in inches, seconds or ounces. You can't plug in a computer to give you the odds if you follow one course as compared with another. There's no attorney by your side to advise you of the legal niceties, nor should there be. The real

question is: What seems best for the mother and child—what is likely to happen if you do this, or don't do that? Your own medical judgment, your knowledge of the patient, all of the signs as you add them up—even your hunches based on past experience—must give you the answer. And you have to act accordingly. You can't postpone the case because all of the evidence isn't in.

Good doctors are anonymous; only their patients know their names unless they happen to write a book or discover a new disease. Will Pickles, a general practitioner serving a rural English community called Wensleydale, is known to us because he wrote a medical classic, *Epidemiology in Country Practice*. The country towns he served were so isolated that he was able to track down all new cases of infectious diseases, and he developed a simple but useful method for charting them. In this he functioned as a public-health doctor, but his interest for us lies in the fact that he was an exemplary clinical doctor, indeed, a beloved doctor. In *Will Pickles of Wensleydale*, biographer John Pemberton reports what Dr. Stephen, a friend of Dr. Pickles, said, "I tried to pick out the secrets of Dr. Pickles's success, and I reached the conclusion that he is a very wise man. He sticks to essentials and to simple principles. He observes exactly and carefully, without any speculative frills. He shows no tendency to jump to unwarranted conclusions. He has persevered in the work over the years. He has recorded his material meticulously, and has been much assisted here by his wife. His general practice has not been too heavy to fatigue him, so that his inquiring spirit has not been dampened." Thus Dr. Pickles is shown to have sapiential authority: he is a wise man.

Dr. Pickles also had great moral authority. Pemberton said of him, "I never heard him disparage a patient. One day a young locum* was reporting on his round to Will, and as he came to each name, it seemed that every patient was either exaggerating his symptoms, was too stupid to carry out the

* A doctor, usually a young doctor, temporarily taking another doctor's place.

treatment advised, or was obviously malingering. The locum seemed to have reprimanded them all. Finally, at the end of the recital, Will, losing his customary urbanity, angrily remarked, 'You *can't* treat these people like that. I've known them for a lifetime—they're *good* people.' " Had the young locum set up practice in Wensleydale, it is not difficult to guess which doctor the patients would have preferred. Patients will not go to a doctor who sees them as immoral if there is a Will Pickles around.

In some ways, the qualities of a good surgeon are even more remarkable than those of a good physician. The patient is often required to make a decision in a single interview about whether or not to trust the surgeon's judgment that the surgery needs to be done, and then that this particular surgeon will perform in the way one would wish during the operation itself. Further decisions may have to be made in the course of surgery depending on what the surgeon finds. The surgeon, then, must be able to convey in a very short time that he is highly competent, excellent at decision-making under difficult conditions, and that he has the patient's best interests at heart. Exactly how good surgeons do this is not known, but it is a fact that they do it, for otherwise no patient would agree to trust his life to a total stranger while he is going to be under an anesthetic.

In Solzhenitsyn's *Cancer Ward*, Dyomka, a young man who faces amputation of his leg, decides he wants to be operated on by Lev Leonidovich, "because however it turned out, whether he saved you or not, it wouldn't be because he'd made a mistake. Of this Dyomka was somehow quite convinced." The author goes on to say, "The intimacy between patient and surgeon is short-lived, but closer than between a son and his own father." Lev Leonidovich had a gift for inspiring confidence in his patients: to one confused patient he said, "What is there for me to say? Our interests are exactly the same. You want to be cured, we want you to be cured, too. Let's carry on in agreement."

Professor James Kirkup wrote a poem after watching a surgeon, Philip Allison, perform a mitral stenosis valvulotomy in the General Infirmary at Leeds. He calls his poem "A Correct Compassion," and it ends:

For this is imagination's other place,
Where only necessary things are done, with supreme and grave
Dexterity that ignores technique; with proper grace
In forming a correct compassion, that performs its loves, and makes
   it live.

Surely that is what we want in a surgeon or a physician: not a sentimental relationship, but a correct compassion.

The good doctor adapts his treatment to the human needs of the particular patient. Kenneth Dewhurst, in his book *Dr. Thomas Sydenham: 1624–1689*, relates how the great doctor sent a depressed patient on a fifteen-hundred-mile horseback journey to see a specialist in the north of Scotland. The man returned very angry because no one had ever heard of the specialist. Sydenham asked about his patient's depression, to which the man replied that it was gone, but no thanks to Dr. Sydenham. Sydenham then asked the patient whether he would have made the trip if he had not believed there was such a specialist, and slowly the man began to realize that the trip itself was the treatment.

The good doctor engages in benign trickery from time to time in order to meet the human but often irrational needs of his patients. The anonymous author of *Confessions of a Gynecologist* had successfully treated a couple for infertility using artificial insemination, but unluckily the wife had miscarried the child. When they returned to try again, this wise doctor collected an ejaculate from the husband and made a considerable ritual of mixing it with the semen of anonymous donors. He says, "In describing the 'new' procedure, it's just possible that I overemphasized the fact that while a single sperm does the actual fertilizing, it needs a lot of help in reaching and preparing the target—and one of Mr. M's sperm might just be the winner in the race. (His sperm count was still quite low but nobody could say that he *couldn't* be the father.)"

The same gynecologist displayed another quality of a good doctor: he tries to keep the costs down for his patients. In treating infertility, he says, "I treat the apparently normal patient in a series of steps, starting with the simple things to hold down costs and avoid making a big complicated deal out of something which may yield to what I call 'commonsense intercourse.' If this doesn't work, we can then go on to more expensive tests and complex procedures."

The exemplary doctor shows respect for other doctors, including doctors of cultures other than his own. According to Sir Henry Stanley in his *Catalogue of an Historical Exhibition*, the famous African explorer, Dr. David Livingstone, was such a man, ". . . one of the sources of his strength in his relations with Africans was his willingness to listen to their arguments about their customs and medical practices. His advice to John Kirk, the medical officer and botanist on the Zambesi Expedition, contained the remark, 'They possess medical men among themselves who are generally the most observant people to be met with. It is desirable to be at all times on good terms with them.' "

The exemplary doctor does not abuse the power Aesculapian authority gives him. In *Lame Deer: Seeker of Visions*, John Lame Deer, a Sioux medicine man, spoke thus of his uncle, Chest:

Chest was an honest man. He never once misused his power. He was an old-fashioned kind of healer, a man from another age. He was never greedy. But there are some conjurers who are fakes and cheats. Maybe some of them have a little power, but they use it in a bad way. . . . But it backfires. A man who misuses his power in this way may see his own children fall sick or even die. The more he gets, the more he loses. You can tell a good medicine man by his actions and his way of life. Is he lean? Does he live in a poor cabin? Does money leave him cold? Does he have a good, loving wife and happy children? Then he is a good medicine man, no matter what methods he uses. It is also a good sign if a man doesn't pretend to be able to cure all sicknesses. If he tells you: "For your ailment, my medicines are no good, but I will send you to somebody who has an herb for you." If he tells you this you know you have spoken to a good man.

In *Reflections of a Medical Investigator*, R. A. McCance, speaking of the Hippocratic oath, said:

The precepts have been analyzed and rewritten many times in accordance with the religious dogmas of the time, but the essence of them is as fresh today as it was when they were first prepared in the Greek Island of Cos in the 5th Century, B.C. In these precepts the doctor undertook to help and treat the sick, but only for their good, never to administer poison or produce abortions even if asked to do so, not to commit adultery, and finally to regard as secret anything which he heard or saw in the course of his practice or in social life outside it, which ought not to be divulged. The code of behavior laid down in these precepts might, I always think, have been written by the patients themselves. They are exactly what the patient looks for, and has always looked for, in his doctor.

Sydenham, called the English Hippocrates, had this to say about the qualifications for a doctor:

It becomes every man who purposes to give himself to the care of others, seriously to consider the four following things: First, that he must one day give an account to the Supreme Judge of all the lives entrusted to his care. Secondly, that all his skill and knowledge, and energy, as they have been given to him by God, so they should be exercised for His glory and the good of mankind, and not for mere gain or ambition. Thirdly, and not more beautifully than truly, let him reflect that he has undertaken the care of no mean creature, for, in order that he may estimate the value, the greatness of the human race, the only begotten son of God became himself a man, and thus ennobled it with His divine dignity, and far more than this, died to redeem it. And fourthly, that the doctor, being himself a mortal man, should be diligent and tender in relieving his suffering patients, inasmuch as he himself must one day be a like sufferer.*

---

* "The Doctor" in *Doctors by Themselves*, Edward F. Griffith, ed.

The doctor Sydenham describes had a rich religious tradition to draw upon, and so was not tempted to play God himself.

Since we go to a doctor in great need, we are inclined to take everything he says seriously. But what if he speaks not from his authority as a doctor, but from his personal prejudices? How does one determine when a doctor is speaking as a doctor and when he is just venting his opinions? Perhaps one should imagine that when a doctor speaks as a doctor, he holds in his hand an imaginary caduceus, that he speaks *cum caduceum*, a medical version of the papal *ex cathedra*.* One can then ask: "Are you speaking *cum caduceum*? Are you speaking as a doctor?" Many silly and annoying things doctors say could thereby be discounted. A good doctor either speaks *cum caduceum* or else lets us know he is speaking as a private citizen.

What are the qualities, then, that make up our composite portrait of the good doctor? He does his best for the patient who has entrusted himself to his care. He has mastered the art of medicine to the best of his ability. He is well disposed toward his patients and generally believes they are trying to tell him what is wrong with them. He does not subscribe to non-medical goals, either for himself or his patient. He either speaks *cum caduceum* or lets you know if he is speaking as a private citizen. Since no doctor knows everything, he does not undermine the efforts of other doctors, although he may hope to do better than they.

The existence of medical impostors is evidence that we know what we want in a doctor when we see it, although we may not be able to describe those qualities accurately in the absence of a real example. A medical impostor is simply someone who understands the doctor role and acts accordingly, although without the educational and legal qualifications which have come to be required. A schoolteacher named Samuel Greenburg became an unwilling impostor

* For this concept we are indebted to Carl Bretz, of Bryce Hospital, Tuscaloosa, Alabama, and for the appropriate Latin term to Ian Mackenzie.

when he went to Japan on a medically sponsored tour in place of his doctor brother-in-law. In an article in *Life* magazine he related his experiences. He was addressed as "doctor," and when he protested, the other doctors and their families made it clear they thought he was trying to evade giving free medical advice. Mr. Greenburg resisted the pressure as long as he could, but then it seemed easier to "admit" that he was a doctor and start consulting with his fellow passengers. He quickly mastered the required role, reassuring one "patient" that "it was nothing serious," listening sympathetically to others, advising some to see various specialists when they got home. To one doctor who recounted his symptoms, he said, "Doctor, what is *your* diagnosis?" The doctor laughed appreciatively and readily diagnosed himself. When asked a technical question he couldn't answer, he said, "You young men are way ahead of my generation." When pressed further about what he would have done in this instance, he gazed off into the distance as if he were recalling a case he had had a long time ago. This had the desired effect; some doctors began to move off, others changed the subject. Later he found he had earned the reputation of a conservative but solid practitioner. Mr. Greenburg found the role so easy and so satisfactory that he signed up for another medical tour. "Somewhere my patients are waiting," he said. One may hazard a guess that "Dr." Greenburg will never be sued for malpractice, for he well understands what is wanted in a doctor.

What attributes do we *not* want in a doctor? What would a medical impostor do his best to avoid? No medical impostor worth his salt would try to seduce a patient—unless that was his sole reason for impostoring. Real doctors know that sexual behavior, however desirable elsewhere, undermines the doctor-patient relationship. Overcharging a patient is something an impostor would want to avoid, for to value money above medical service casts doubt on the authenticity of Aesculapian authority. Doctors may appear affluent—

presumably from seeing many patients and taking difficult cases—but they must not appear greedy.

A too-great delight in technical expertise ("Now just let me show you this wonderful new machine I have here") gives patients the uneasy feeling that they may become mere playthings of a gadget-happy doctor. Technical virtuosity may be greatly appreciated when needed, but no one wants to feel the doctor has been waiting for just such a case on which to try out his new whatsis. Amateur psychoanalysis is not appreciated by patients, for it suggests the doctor is covering up deficiencies in medical knowledge, so the canny impostor would do well to stick to medical considerations. Too much interest in hustling elderly patients toward the grave tends to cast doubt on a doctor's true calling. Perhaps the doctor has an interest in a funeral parlor! The general rule is very simple: the doctor—or the impostor—must appear to be applying his knowledge solely for the benefit of the patient. That is what tells us we are talking to a real doctor—or a real impostor.

In addition to the clinical doctor, with his virtues, his vices, and his impostors, there are two other legitimate roles for doctors to occupy, the public-health doctor and the science doctor.* The public-health doctor is responsible for maintaining the health of a given population. We meet him mostly on the pages of our newspapers: "Doctors Weigh Dangers of Swine Flu Inoculations," "Restaurant Closed by Board of Health," "Doctors Investigate Mysterious New Disease in Africa." Public-health doctors do not have Aesculapian authority, and we relate to them as citizen to official, not as patient to doctor. They have structural authority, which is vested in the position they occupy and not in themselves. Unlike clinical doctors or science doctors, they can actually give orders. But they can do this only with regard to

---

* For a more complete account of the three kinds of doctors, see the chapter, "Medicine and Its Submodels," in our book *Models of Madness, Models of Medicine*.

matters which involve a high degree of public consensus, as in the control of smallpox and typhoid fever. Where there is a lesser degree of consensus—as with swine flu inoculations or the dangers of smoking—they can only give advice, which we can choose to disregard.

Some doctors act as both clinical and public health doctors, especially in small communities such as Dr. Pickles's Wensleydale. There is no problem with this as long as the doctor knows which "hat" he is wearing.

The science doctor plays the role of scientific investigator to the patient's role of experimental subject. He tries to learn about diseases in a systematic and replicable way. Having neither the Aesculapian authority of the clinical doctor nor the structural authority of the public-health doctor, the science doctor's authority is only sapiential. In order to get experimental subjects, he must woo them, inspire their cooperation in his research effort, and when he gets them, he can give them neither medical advice nor legal orders.

Some doctors can act as both a science doctor and a clinical doctor. A famous example of such a doctor is William Beaumont. In 1822, Alexis St. Martin sustained a gunshot wound which left a hole in his abdominal wall. The young trapper was thought to be dying, but Dr. Beaumont successfully nursed him back to life and took complete care of him for two years. Then Beaumont formally engaged the young man as a research subject and during the next eleven years performed 238 experiments on him, the results of which were reported in *Experiments and Observations on the Gastric Juice and the Physiology of Digestion*, a medical classic. Beaumont shifted deftly back and forth between the two roles, stopping the experiments and doctoring St. Martin when he became ill, resuming the experiments when St. Martin agreed to it. This well-documented case shows that it is possible for a doctor to be both a clinical doctor to his patient and a scientific investigator to his subject without damaging the *swanelo* of either role.

We once knew a doctor who played all three roles. During the day he was a science doctor, studying leukemia in a laboratory. Evenings and weekends he had a tiny private practice in the small town where he lived. Once a month, he convened the town's board of health, of which he was president. As the science doctor, he displayed his special knowledge in scientific papers and meetings. As the public-health doctor, he once closed the town's nursery school because of an encephalitis epidemic. As the clinical doctor, he treated the particular, individual patients who came to him. He was much esteemed by his scientific colleagues, his fellow townspeople, and his patients, and he never, never put on the wrong hat.

There are a limited number of roles open to doctors or healers, and they have a very long history. The clinical doctor can manifest himself as shaman, medicine man, or folk healer. Sometimes he appears as a more frightening figure: that of the sorcerer. The sorcerer is a healer believed to have unlimited magic powers of life and death over his patients. His power directly reflects the degree of his patients' fears, from which he promises to deliver them—sometimes by protecting them from the spells of other sorcerers. Whenever, in our desire to have total magical protection, we endow someone with total power, we have called in the sorcerer.

Every doctor has a potential sorcerer within him. It is up to the patient not to release that potential, for here lies the origin of our fear and hatred of doctors. We realize that anyone whose magic is strong enough to protect us from the evil of illness can also use his strength against us.

How do we keep the doctor where we want him, powerful enough to help us but contained enough so his powers are used only on our behalf? We do this by constricting his role so it is always complementary to our role as patient. We must question, then, our perverse habit of encouraging and even demanding that doctors expand their role. Currently, we want them to be more interested in death, dying, and matters beyond the grave; in prevention, nutrition, and population control; in social justice, scientific research, and administration. We want our doctors to be "holistic," but have we asked ourselves what it would really be like if our doctors were interested in every aspect of our beings? Do we really want them to be concerned with our souls as well as our bodies? How about our life-styles, our religious and spiritual beliefs, our political ideologies?

Ibsen created a holistic doctor, Tomas Stockmann, in his play, *A Public Enemy*. Dr. Stockmann went from being a country practitioner to the director of the public baths in his native town. Declaring the baths to be polluted (which was his duty as a public-health officer), he went on to say that the spiritual life of the community was even more polluted and that he would set it right. The townspeople grew more and more alarmed at this sorcerer-doctor whom they had conjured up, and in the end they turned against him and called him "an enemy of the people." Beware of any doctor who yearns to treat the body politic instead of real, individual patients. He is on his way to becoming a sorcerer.

Our fear of doctors is well-founded, but so is our love. There is no tenderer relationship than that between a doctor with correct compassion and his sick patient. No matter that it is all forgotten the instant our health is regained; the doctor will have other patients and we will find our way back when we need him again.

XI *Doctors as Patients*

DOCTORS MAKE TERRIBLE PATIENTS; everybody knows that. But why? Surely doctors, with their special knowledge, have advantages over lay patients who can only guess what is wrong with them. Alas for doctors, it does not work that way. Medical knowledge is of value only to a *patient*. There is nothing more difficult for a doctor to do than to transform himself into a patient, for to do this he must divest himself of Aesculapian authority—which he does not want to do and does not know how to do.

Dr. Samuel Zelman tells us how not to do it. In "The Case of the Perilous Prune Pit," he says, "A forty-five-year-old physician, who might reasonably be expected to know better, thoughtlessly swallowed a prune pit one morning at breakfast . . . and promptly forgot the matter completely." After six or seven weeks of inexplicable pain, Dr. Zelman diagnosed a duodenal ulcer and gave up drinking coffee, but to no avail. "The patient, who apparently never considered consulting a physician, next attributed his symptoms to an irritable bowel." Now he changed to a bland diet, again without results. After palpating his own abdomen, and then frantically hunting through the medical textbooks, he opted for a tumor, "The patient demanded an immediate radiologic study of the small bowel, to be followed without delay by surgical intervention." Fortunately for the patient—Dr. Zelman—the prune pit passed through his system and into the municipal sewers before any damage was done. Dr. Zelman refers to himself as "the patient," but the truth is he failed to give up the role of the doctor, and, as the saying goes, he who is his own doctor has a fool for a physician, and another for a patient.

Dr. Zelman got off with merely feeling foolish, but Professor Kerppola, an eminent Finnish physician, did himself in with his confusion of the sick role, the doctor role, and the dying role. According to his daughter, also a physician, Dr. Kerppola was hospitalized at the age of eighty-three for severe back pain. In theory, he was under the care of a physician who had once been his student, but actually, he never relinquished his own Aesculapian authority. He would not allow any diagnostic work-up because he had concluded from his own observations that he had an incurable disease. Without any further fuss, he placed himself immovably in the dying role. After five months in the hospital, he died. An autopsy, which he had requested in order to reveal the "final" truth, showed that he had treatable cancer of the prostate. Dr. B. J. Kennedy, commenting on Dr. Kerppola's death in an article in the *Journal of the American Medical Association,* said:

Not to have imposed a few simple diagnostic tests and a few milligrams of estrogenic hormone resulted in the tragic loss of a life, probably prematurely. The conventional treatment of carcinoma of the prostate is not new, not "inhumane," and well within the realm of what every physician should provide a patient. Although everyone should have a right to die and to involve himself in the decision-making, it does seem a tragedy when a patient with cancer undergoes a painful phase of dying whereas treatment might have prevented this distress, possibly allowing death to occur later from sudden vascular disease. This is an outstanding example in which the diagnosis would have been of value and in my opinion, it was not "in the best interests of the patient to abandon the search for it."

Evidently both Dr. Kerppola's former student and his daughter were bamboozled by the indomitable old man's Aesculapian authority. The ex-student allowed Dr. Kerppola to assume the rights of the sick role (five months of high-level medical care in a hospital) without having to undertake any of its duties, and then to place himself in the dying role without the agreement of those caring for him. His daughter was persuaded to publish this account of her father's death— also in the *Journal of the American Medical Association*—as an example of "death with dignity," but it serves better as an example of a gross misuse of Aesculapian authority to the extreme detriment of the doctor-patient holding it and of those who loved and respected him. The old professor also managed to usurp the Aesculapian authority of his own doctor and his daughter without their recognizing what had happened.

Sometimes a doctor, finding himself ill, applies for the sick role in good faith, only to find that his doctors continue to treat him as a colleague rather than as a patient. This was the complaint of Dr. Max Pinner, a physician with heart disease, in *When Doctors Are Patients:*

Because I am a physician myself, not more than one or two of my physicians were able (nor did they even make a reasonable attempt) to avoid discussing my "case" with me as if I had been called into consultation. They failed to give definite orders and advice and tended to say, explicitly or implicitly, "You know what to do!" But even if I did know, such an attitude fails to give the psychic relief that every patient expects from his physician. The assumption "that I knew" was once carried so far that my surgeon indicated in the nurse's order book that I would prescribe for myself, immediately after a major operation and during a period when I had brief episodes of disorientation. And, be it stressed, I had begged each one of my physicians to treat me just like any other patient and to forget that I had any medical knowledge.

Dr. Pinner was mistaken in supposing that his medical knowledge was the problem. It was his Aesculapian authority that his doctors were unable to forget. He should have told his doctors that in this circumstance his own Aesculapian authority was a burden and a danger to him and that he would have to rely on theirs, as would any other patient.

One doctor found himself a patient in his own hospital after an automobile accident in which he sustained a concussion and cerebral contusion. In spite of his injuries, he kept up appearances so well that his colleagues believed him when he said there was nothing wrong with him. Fortunately, his wife realized he was far from normal and got his colleagues to agree—or so she thought. On visiting him one day, she was dismayed to find him closeted with a colleague discussing three especially difficult patients at great length. Her husband was offering medical advice with his usual detachment and aplomb. However, he now has no idea whether his advice was sound, because he cannot remember anything about it. Eventually, he realized how ill he was and the situation was normalized. His Aesculapian authority, which in almost any other circumstance would have been an asset, was in this instance a potentially lethal liability. Sick doctors are in danger not only of medical neglect, and their own efforts at self-treatment, but may even be asked to treat other patients as well. Even the worst-treated patient is not expected to do this.

We were recently told of a doctor, the head of a prestigious medical school department, who sustained a heart attack and was hospitalized. A colleague reports that after three days, he was "clamoring for his briefcase," and also much annoyed that the staff called him "Mr. A." instead of "Dr. A." He then dismissed himself from the hospital against medical advice and resumed his heavy program. Very soon he was back in the hospital with pneumonia. Now he is out again, holding court at home. It remains to be seen how long he survives his own inept patienthood.

One of the worst aspects of this case is that the doctor's outrageous and self-destructive behavior, which in anyone else would have raised questions about his mental competence, was seen as merely amiable eccentricity on his part, and a source of amusement for his friends and colleagues. So far as we know, no one who knows him or works with him is eager to attend his funeral, but that is exactly what will happen unless they all stop being amused and exert the same moral pressure on him that they would on any non-medical person. Much responsibility lies with his doctors in the hospital, who ought to have fought fire with fire, and pitted their Aesculapian authority against his. It says much for the perplexing effect of Dr. A.'s own Aesculapian authority that this evidently did not happen.

Dr. William Nolen, a surgeon who needed surgery for coronary artery disease, noted the special hazards of being a doctor-turned-patient. Although he was in most respects an exemplary patient, there was a weak link in his patienthood. As he stated in his book, *Surgeon Under the Knife*, "To put it succinctly, when it came to blood pressure control, I behaved like an idiot. I might add here that my doctors let me get away with this. Instead of chewing me out, insisting that I take better care of myself—as they would if I were a layman—they let me guide myself. Another example of that very common phenomenon—the doctor who doesn't always get optimum medical care."

Dr. Nolen was deeply impressed with the experience of being on the receiving end of Aesculapian authority. When he went into a local hospital to have an angiogram, the surgeon told him he would probably need surgery after the test and advised him to pick a surgeon. Dr. Nolen and his wife were quite unprepared for this and, not wishing to be rushed into such an important decision, decided to leave the hospital without the angiogram. Dr. Nolen later wondered what he would have done had he not been a physician himself, "Here I am, a surgeon, with a reasonably complete knowledge of what by-passes are all about, and I almost went along with him. Sometimes I think all doctors, and I include myself, don't realize what authoritative figures we are. We take our power for granted and we shouldn't." Here Dr. Nolen comes very close to stating explicitly that doctors know little or nothing about their own authority. Only the experience of being a patient called this to his attention.

Being a physician did not save Dr. Nolen from the all-too-familiar miseries and errors of being a hospital patient. While waiting hungrily in bed for a blood test that had to be done before he could eat his breakfast, Dr. Nolen learned that the blood had been drawn from the man in the next room by mistake, who also happened to be a doctor. That puzzled patient's blood had gone down to the laboratory with Dr. Nolen's name on it! Five times during his preoperative period in the hospital Dr. Nolen found errors in his medication. Of course, he recognized most of the pills and knew what he should be taking, but he believes every patient should ask the doctor what he should be getting and how often and then check the actual pills against those prescribed.

Dr. Nolen found being "prepped" for his operation an unnecessarily miserable experience. The orderly did not show up until eleven P.M. He failed to complete the necessary shaving and neglected to give the prescribed enema, so it was 12:30 before someone else was found to do this. The nurse then gave him some painful antibiotic shots which interfered with his sleep (as did the belated enema). It was one A.M. before a resident could be found to write an order for pain medication. Dr. Nolen had hoped for a full night's sleep to prepare himself for the rigors of the operation itself.

As doctor-turned-patient, Dr. Nolen made a very important discovery: he cared more about his own health and safety than any doctor or nurse possibly could. "I have taken care of thousands of patients in my professional career, and though I think I am at least as compassionate and concerned about my patients as the average physician, I know I never worried about one of them as intensely as I, as a patient, worried about myself." Only a doctor-patient could have brought us this particular observation, and its implications are far-reaching: the doctor must avoid playing God and thus deceiving himself and his patient about his concern and his powers, and the patient must take more responsibility for what happens to him, since no one can care about him as much as he cares about himself. This is Nolen's Principle, and it means that doctors have the duty to encourage people to be responsible patients, to do what they can to help themselves. This is quite different from Kerppola's Principle: that only the sick doctor knows enough to prescribe for himself.

A number of doctor-patients have been surprised to find how difficult it is to communicate the subjective experience of being ill. Dr. Max Samter, who suffered from deafness, said, "My own chief complaint was the ringing in the ears (tinnitus), which had become loud and unceasing; it drowned out relaxed thought and concentration. I was disturbed by the fact that tinnitus escaped detection by objective means; especially that no one 'knew how I felt.' "*

A similar observation was made by Dr. Merritt Low, who was recovering from an attack of polio, "Having been a patient, it is now possible for me to understand how sick people become focused on their gastrointestinal tract beyond all reason and common sense, while physicians often neglect such symptoms beyond all reason and common sense." Dr. Low goes on to say, "There is a psychic as well as a physical narrowing, which takes place in a long acute illness, of which

*This and the following examples of doctors as patients are from *When Doctors Are Patients,* edited by Max Pinner and Benjamin Miller.

not all are aware. The patient himself may even believe and convince others, that he is greatly interested in the outside world—but often he isn't. The true broadening of his narrowed world accompanies and also mutually stimulates recovery. The patient takes refuge in unbelievable rigidities of routine, any irregularities in which lead to great irritability and frustration. Even carefree and casual individuals outcrotchet the crotchety. I don't know the reason for this except that all one's feeble energies seem directed toward a personal situation when there isn't much margin for other thoughts. . . . All illness is, of course, both mental and physical."

Martin Grotjahn, a psychoanalyst, in writing of his experience in passing a small kidney stone, said, "The renal colics were not the worst; they could be tolerated, or controlled if need be by narcotics. More agonizing were the slow, grinding, peristaltic movements of the ureter which were not so painful or so easily diagnosed as the dramatic colics. They felt like 'vegetative storms' and appeared embarrassingly hysterical, anxious and tense. They soon made me feel like an hysteric. In this condition, the specialists were not of much help. They saw that the kidney stone was moving slowly along its predestined way. They could not understand my complaints, and were obviously delighted to look for psychological reasons for my 'hypochondriasis.' " This particular doctor was in double jeopardy as a patient: not only was he a doctor, but he was a doctor who did not normally confer the sick role, belonging as he did to the aberrant sub-speciality of psychoanalysis. To his great relief, he finally found a doctor who was not given to psychological explanations and who told him exactly what was happening and that all his discomfort was expected. "To be understood in these terms without psychology and psychoanalysis, without being made ridiculous or threatened by operation, gave me such relief that I passed the stone within twenty-four hours." Dr. Grotjahn later learned that the source of this doctor's wisdom was his own experience as a patient with kidney stones.

Dr. Fredric Wertham, a psychiatrist with thrombophlebitis, wrote about experiencing pain, "Strange though it may seem, we physicians are apt not to acknowledge the tragedy of pain. Even though I no longer remember clearly my pain experience, I still have with me the realization that it is easier to be philosophical about death than about pain. Death is the transition from biochemistry to chemistry; but one can't make wisecracks about pain. As scientific physicians, we want to find causes, trace processes, cure and prevent. But every patient who comes to us has at the back of his mind a simple and what you might call primitive or infantile wish: he wants the doctor to alleviate his pain and banish his fear."

Sick doctors not only learn to appreciate the vast subjective side of illness; they even learn to appreciate nurses! Julius Gottlieb wrote, "Physicians generally appreciate the value of care provided by good nurses, but never before was I completely conscious of their full merit. Their companionship and cheering greetings were mentally stimulating. A hand ever ready to assist in turning over, the sponge and alcohol bath, the gentle and firm massage to bring tone to flabby muscles, the rubdown of the back to relieve fatigue, the confidence inspired by timely medication and presentation of necessary nourishment—these are the experiences that only a patient learns to value fully." Thus do doctors learn what patients already know.

Do physicians believe they become better doctors for having been ill themselves? Dr. Ian Stevenson thinks they do, "Certainly one's sensitivity to the feelings of others is greatly enhanced, and this can become a rich asset to the physician. There is, on the physical plane, an increased understanding of symptoms which for the patient are so difficult to describe and for the healthy physician so hard to appreciate. There is also an awareness of subtle, ill-defined sensations of malaise which the patient is frequently unable to convey to his physician but which make up a large part of his symptomatic complaints. The physician who has himself been sick is alert to detect the fluctuations in the well-being of the patient which accompany changes in physical state and mood, each of which is reflected in the other." Norman Goldsmith, a physician who had multiple sclerosis, said, "I know that I am a far better physician, more sympathetic and more understanding of all the difficulties of patients, than I was before I became ill."

Patienthood comes as a great surprise to doctors. While we don't wish they get ill, we do appreciate it when they understand their patients better for having been ill themselves. For those doctors who have never been hospitalized, we have to communicate the subjective aspects of illness so they will really hear us.

How do doctors rate in patienthood? They do better than their patients when it is a question of having medical knowledge, as Dr. Nolen demonstrated. They will easily spot errors in medication, and they are more likely to refuse a course of action which does not seem right. As for communicating the subjective aspects of illness or making themselves comfortable in hospitals, they seem to do no better than the rest of us—which certainly calls into question any theory of medicine as a conspiracy among doctors to cheat patients. When it comes to accepting or acquiring the sick role, they do much worse. Either they cannot or will not jettison their Aesculapian authority or else their colleagues insist on relating to them as doctors rather than patients. This is the most serious problem doctors face in their quest for good medical care.

Doctors who need doctors are in worse shape than lawyers who need lawyers, for the latter involves only sapiential authority. The doctor's doctor is somewhat like the pope's confessor, except the church is explicit and medicine isn't. It is understood that being the pope's confessor is a special role, and therefore a special priest is chosen and trained for this job. It is recognized that papal authority is liable to bias the confessor and spiritual advisor, who is especially fortified so that he can cope with those difficulties which might and probably have arisen. Pope and confessor are both aware that each has a different authority and both know the limits of their own and the other's authority.

The medical situation is utterly different. Hardly any doctor even knows the name of the medical authority or has given much thought to its nature. Due to the confounding presence of Aesculapian authority, good doctors are likely to become confused and unsure about the role relationships involved, and so the sick doctor may not get the best treatment. Unlike their patients, who only have to beware of bad doctors, doctors themselves may be in danger from admirable colleagues who in other circumstances would treat a nondoctor skillfully and adroitly.

Perhaps doctors who acquire a working knowledge of Aesculapian authority may wish to have a little card or plaque in their offices for the doctor-patients: Doctors, please leave your Aesculapian authority in the waiting room. Doctors becoming patients should reassure their colleagues that "I have left my Aesculapian authority with your nurse or secretary."* It is very important for the doctor who is ill to acquire the sick role because there is a great difference between a treating doctor who is consulting with a colleague and the one who is treating a patient.

It is very much in our interest to keep our doctors alive and well, and we can hardly afford to invest in their lengthy education if they are going to endanger their lives and even kill themselves off through the inept use of Aesculapian authority. As prudent patients, we must insist that our doctors learn about the nature of their authority, especially how to get rid of it when they need to transform themselves from doctors into patients. Both out of humanity and self-interest, we want our doctors to have the sick role when they need it,

---

*For these suggestions we are indebted to Carl Bretz of Bryce Hospital, Tuscaloosa, Alabama.

so that when we get sick, they will be in shape to confer upon us this life-saving role.

All of us invest in the education of our doctors, through city, county, state, and federal taxes, as well as church and private donations. What kind of return do we get on our investment? Doctors often die young, presumably from overwork, but also, we would contend, from inept patienthood. Poor patienthood is an avoidable evil, and it is very much in our interest, both selfish and humane, to see that our doctors get the very best medical care. This they can do, as all of us must, by practicing responsible patienthood.

Alternative Roles

XII *The "Psych" Role*

THE SICK ROLE has a sister role which was recognized by us some years ago and named the "psych" role.* This role is assigned to a wide variety of troubled, unhappy, conflicted, unfulfilled, or even curious and enquiring people who are seeking or engaged in some kind of psychotherapy. The sick role and the "psych" role are usually distinguishable once it is understood that it is essential to differentiate between them. Failure to recognize the differences result in a person getting the sick role when he needs the "psych" role, and vice versa. Mistakes of this kind are always harmful and can be fatal. There are times when one may need and ought to occupy both roles because one is both sick and troubled; the question then is how to occupy both roles at the same time.

Some of the confusion between the sick role and the

* This concept was presented by us under the title "Some Differences Between the Sick Role and the 'Psych' Role" at the American Society for Psychosomatic Dentistry and Medicine, October 6, 1972, Mt. Pocono, Pennsylvania.

"psych" role is derived from the long and complicated history of psychoanalysis. Troubled people occupied this role, or something like it, long before Freud, but it was Freud's development of psychoanalysis as a *medical treatment* which produced the muddle which continues to this day. In 1911, Freud considered psychoanalysis to be a brief medical treatment for diseases called psychoneuroses. He was explicit about this and in a letter to Ernest Jones found in Aubrey Lewis's *The State of Psychiatry* shows that he subscribed to the medical model:

> We are to withstand the big temptation to settle down in our colonies, where we cannot but be strangers, distinguished visitors, and have to revert every time to our native country in Medicine, where we find the roots of our powers.

Freud recognized that a "big temptation" existed, but still he accepted psychoanalysis as part of medicine. Had the concept existed in 1911, Freud might have written: We must maintain our Aesculapian authority in order to treat patients in the sick role.

By 1927, Freud was abandoning the medical model just as explicitly as he had asserted the need for it sixteen years earlier. At this time psychoanalysis had begun to include growing numbers of people who were to have a profound effect upon it. These were analysts-in-training and artists or writers; they were not ill, were not in the sick role, and could not be called patients. Indeed a new word, psychoanalysand, was invented to describe the new role. At this same time the success of psychoanalysis as a medical treatment was being questioned by Freud himself.

In 1927, Freud made his strongest, but unsuccessful, attempt to dissolve the bonds between medicine and psychoanalysis. His views, stated in *The Question of Lay Analysis* and in a letter to Paul Federn, leaves no doubt of his intention. The full significance of this unsuccessful attempt to cut the umbilical cord with medicine was not understood because neither the sick role nor the "psych" role existed in 1927. It was not possible to gauge just what would occur if the switch from the one role to the other was made by psychoanalysts, many of whom were physicians and therefore possessed or were possessed by Aesculapian authority. In *The Question of Lay Analysis* Freud wrote:

> It will not have escaped my readers that in what I have said I have assumed as axiomatic something that is still violently disputed in the discussion. I have assumed, that is to say, that psychoanalysis is not a specialized branch of medicine. I cannot see how it is possible to dispute this. . . . The possibility of its application to medical purposes must not lead us astray.

And lest there by any possible doubt, there are Freud's remarks to Paul Federn in the same year:

> The battle for lay analysis must, at one time or another, be fought to the finish. Better now than later. As long as I live I shall resist that psychoanalysis be swallowed up by medicine.*

What, then, is the "psych" role that is applied to the role held by the psychoanalysand who is not a patient and is not in the sick role? There are and have been from the start two aspects of the "psych" role which must be understood. First, the role became differentiated from the sick role because psychoanalysts-in-training, artists, and writers who were not patients wanted to be psychoanalyzed. Second, the goal of the role holder ceased to be that of recovering health or halting illness. The new goals included an increase of happiness or at least equanimity, becoming more creative, enlightened, or mature. These goals are not usually associated with recovery from illness, where one is expected to be satisfied with just feeling better and being restored to one's previous level of functioning.

As with the sick role, those seeking the "psych" role who feel unhappy, frustrated, or unfulfilled often seek help and

---

*From "How Freudian Are the Freudians?" by Ernest Federn.

counsel from family members who frequently cope successfully with minor distresses and upsets just as they handle
minor illness. Should the family fail, the person seeking relief or enlightenment may approach friends, neighbors,
teachers, or the clergy, all of whom can be helpful. Finally, he
or she may enlist the services of a great variety of psychotherapists. These are professional people who confer the
"psych" role and provide whatever version of that role they
consider beneficial for that particular person.

It should be evident that those who occupy the "psych"
role, or plan to do so, require an even clearer grasp of the nature of the role than those who are in the sick role. Not only
must the role holder be very sure about the rights and duties
involved, but he must make certain that the therapist shares
his views. We hope this book will make it possible for those
in the sick role to be equally circumspect, but the sick role is
so universal and so widely cross-cultural that there is likely
to be some consensus among those involved in the role. Yet
even here, all kinds of misunderstandings occur. The
"psych" role, being more attached to particular cultures, is
subject to greater uncertainties and ambiguities. What is
more, the goals of this role are far more variable than those of
the sick role; they can range from a wish to resolve troubling
thoughts and feelings to hopes of securing the best possible
performance in life.

The "psych" role differs from the sick role in its rights and
duties, its *swanelo*. Unlike the sick role, it carries little in the
way of exemption from normal responsibilities, perhaps because there is less distinction between troubled and un-
troubled people than there is between sick and healthy people. From time to time all of us are troubled. Many religions
consider life a vale of tears and some believe it is an illusion;
consequently we are less willing to exempt others or ourselves from the usual duties for so subjective a matter as
unhappiness than we are for illness which is commonly more
ascertainable.

In both the sick role and the "psych" role it is improper to blame others for one's condition, and it is extremely improper for a doctor or therapist to do so. Yet psychological troubles often have an obvious origin in the afflicted person's family background, and had the family acted differently, their offspring might never have needed therapy. The wise therapist allows the "patient" (who is better called client, counselee, or even analysand, for he or she is not in the sick role and so cannot be a patient) to express anger or dissatisfaction about the family without letting him escape from being fully responsible for the way he feels and lives now.

In both the sick and the "psych" roles, the patient or client has a duty to try to get well as quickly as possible, but the moral imperative to do so is far stronger in the sick role. Since the "psych" role seldom involves abandoning one's usual role and fewer indulgences are permitted, there is less urgency to relinquish it. Indeed, occupying the "psych" role may interfere so little with everyday life that perhaps only a few intimates may even be aware therapy is in progress.

Psychotherapy is sometimes considered a kind of education, even a form of higher education; it can become a long-continuing process, which is not very different from that search for self-understanding and self-enlightenment to which some people devote most of their lives. The more psychotherapy resembles a quest for enlightenment, the less it resembles the sick role. The more it is being done to resolve a particular crisis, the more it resembles the sick role and the more likely that the two will be confused.

Most of us feel that if someone is very sick he ought to seek medical help. So strong is this imperative, that the state sometimes pits itself against families who, for religious or other reasons, refuse medical treatment for their children. Few of us harbor such strong feelings about the need for psychotherapy, so there is little moral pressure to undertake the "psych" role. However, there are those who believe that psychotherapy will resolve many of life's problems, and they try

to encourage their friends and relatives to "get into therapy."
In the early days of psychoanalysis and for some decades af-
terwards psychoanalysands were inclined to importune others, much like those newly converted to a religion. These
proselytes were sometimes absurd and even offensive.
Others feel very differently; they feel that only weaklings
need to spend hours (even fifty-minute hours) chattering
self-indulgently about those problems which we must all endure. The amount of pressure a troubled person receives either from himself or others to undertake therapy of some
kind reflects his social status, background, and life-style
rather than the seriousness of his problems. Those of higher
social class who are removed from ethnic and religious ties
are most likely to accept therapy as a relief from their difficulties. Indeed, there are some enclaves of people among whom
not being in therapy is considered aberrant.

The sick person who does not cooperate in medical treatment is threatened, sometimes explicity, with death. "You'll
die if you don't take your medicine" or "You must have the
operation now to save your life." The uncooperative patient
is left with little doubt as to the horrors in store for him. But
psychotherapy has a name for lack of cooperation: resistance.
In some kinds of psychotherapy, the resolution of resistance
is the centerpiece of the therapy, not just a nuisance or a
suicidal lack of medical piety.

Thus the sick role is the stronger role, with much broader
social consensus. But does this mean that psychological problems are less serious than physical ones? As we have shown
in this book, many people live full lives facing serious and
even fatal illnesses bravely. Others, whose health seems excellent, have their lives ruined by unresolved and untreated
psychological problems. So although the "psych" role seldom
receives the massive social support given so readily to those
in the sick role, for a particular person its acquisition may be
vitally important. Since these two roles are so easily confused, it is essential to learn how to differentiate them.

One of the worst results of a medical interview is to be offered the "psych" role instead of the sick role. Why should it be such a devastating experience to be told by a doctor that "it's all in your mind"? One might suppose this would be good news, for it is always possible to change one's mind and psychotherapy is usually less painful and less dangerous than medical treatment. However, if someone has the slightest suspicion that he indeed has a physical illness he knows instinctively that the "psych" role cannot give sufficient support. It does not help in obtaining the necessary medical treatment and does not give one the strength to accept it. To make matters worse, when a doctor, the very person whose task it is to confer the sick role, denies us that role, much distress and anxiety is generated. The implication must be that the supposedly sick person is exaggerating or possibly malingering. In the face of the subjective experience of still feeling ill, the would-be patient may fear for his life.

On the other hand, those seeking the "psych" role may be given the sick role by mistake. For instance, a woman who wants to discuss some family matter with her husband may be fobbed off with "Oh, you're just pre-menstrual!" Or someone approaching a psychiatrist hoping for a psychotherapeutic relationship may receive a tranquillizer instead. The psychiatrist may assume the patient seeks relief from symptoms, which is reasonable enough when he or she is in the sick role but not necessarily helpful to someone seeking to resolve some problem of human relationships.

It is often a mistake to expect physicians to give someone the "psych" role unless, as with some psychoanalysts, they devote themselves solely to therapy. When dealing with a doctor, one is likely to end up in the sick role or in some confused version of the two roles. Furthermore, there is no reason to pay medical fees for a service which is not medical. Most therapists—psychologists, social workers, marriage counselors—are not physicians, and most physicians are not therapists.

Those who seek and receive the "psych" role from a physician may encounter even graver problems. Aesculapian authority acquires its legitimacy only in relationship to the sick role. It is the presence of the patient, the sick-role holder, who focuses the doctor's behavior, preventing it from becoming arbitrary, capricious, or even outrageous. Psychiatrists and other doctors, too, get into trouble because the boundaries of the "psych" role are poorly marked. A well-known example of this is provided by the disagreement between Freud and Ferenczi about a new technique which the latter was introducing. Ferenczi indicated that by fondling and embracing patients in psychoanalysis he might provide them with the mothering they had missed earlier in life. According to Ernest Jones's *The Life and Work of Sigmund Freud*, this lead Freud to ask, "Why stop at a kiss?" Psychiatrists have been known to use "therapeutic seduction" as a treatment for some patients, and one patient in New York successfully sued because of this. We have even heard of instances where patients sued not because of the "therapeutic seduction" itself, but only because they were billed for it at the usual rate.

If a doctor is treating a patient, seduction is not only forbidden, it is inexcusable; but the rules governing the "psych" role are far from clear. If the "psych" role is, as has often been suggested, an educational role, then we are concerned with a pupil-teacher relationship. Seduction of a pupil by a teacher may, as in the case of Heloise and Abelard, be much resented by the family, but it is not and has never been totally forbidden. Professors who make love to their pupils may be viewed with envy or dislike by their peers, but such behavior is seldom considered utterly reprehensible. As for the beloved pupil, he or she may not only get better grades, but may benefit greatly from the combined relationship. This is not true of the doctor-patient relationship, where the patient's life may be forfeit when the relationship changes to that of doctor-lover. It has long been recognized that doctors who are affectively involved lose their objectivity, that is why doctors are warned against treating members of their own families.

Doctors are used to taking drastic action to benefit gravely ill patients, so when similar situations appear in the "psych" role the physician-therapist is likely to suggest major changes in the patient's life and life-style, which may not be wise or necessary. It is not easy to resist "doctor's orders" because of the weight of Aesculapian authority and the piety which it generates. If a physician advises that divorce is needed as "treatment," he is likely to receive more careful attention than a non-physician giving the same advice.

A more common problem occurs when a patient knows he is not benefiting from psychotherapy, but because of the power of Aesculapian authority and the uncertainty of its limits in the absence of illness, he cannot terminate the relationship. This results in prolonged, unsuccessful treatment, which is less likely to occur in the sick role where, once the patient feels well, the doctor's authority vanishes. If treatment does not succeed in the sick role, one is expected to find another doctor. This is not true of the "psych" role because it is seldom clear when therapy should end and whether it ever will. Freud recognized this when he wrote that psychoanalysis was "terminable and interminable." What were originally the goals of therapy may be achieved, only to reveal others in need of resolution. Aesculapian authority is not well suited for long-standing, slowly changing situations, and the doctor who is not slighted sometimes becomes overbearing and dictatorial. Those with Aesculapian authority should think twice before conferring the "psych" role and removing the sick role.

There is another reason why doctors should hesitate to confer the "psych" role and why patients should decide whether they want to be moved out of the sick role. The "psych" role is holistic: the therapist must try to see the patient as a whole person; everything in his or her life is inter-

esting and potentially important. The most intimate relationships, his family of origin, the schooling he has had, the
work he has done, his social class and ethnic background are
all of the greatest interest to the therapist because they reflect
the client's attitudes toward himself and toward therapy.
Fears from the past and hopes for the future are all grist to
the therapeutic mill. The therapist is concerned with per-
sonhood, not patienthood.

The doctor sees things differently. He tries to *rule out* data
not immediately relevant to reaching a diagnosis. Like an in-
vestigative scientist and a good detective, a doctor becomes
very skilled at sifting through and sorting out a large number
of variables in a short time. And some variables (such as
temperature, blood pressure, white-blood count, blood-cal-
cium level, loss of appetite, severe depression) are more important than others. They all share the rare ability to avoid
"taking everything into account." All three concentrate upon
those things most likely to solve the case.

The client receiving psychotherapy is rightly dismayed if
the therapist is only interested in some narrow slice of life
and neglects its totality. The medical patient, on the other
hand, is greatly reassured when the doctor knows exactly
what minute segments of his total experience are relevant to
his illness. The doctor may concentrate his whole attention
upon the insignificant fact that a small mole has gotten a little
larger and is occasionally bleeding, for this is an early warning of a potentially deadly melanoma and the sooner it is
spotted the better.

Illness tests our resources of intelligence, courage, imagination, and detachment to their limits. What most of us need
is a simple, straightforward, brief account of our illness and
then to be told what can be done about it. Even the most
egotistical person finds a full scale biography and assessment
of the whole person does little good and may do harm at this
juncture. It uses up more time and energy than can be af-
forded. The sick role is, as one would expect, well suited to

the needs of ill people. The "map" of the illness provided by this role hardly ever bears much resemblance to the "whole truth" about that particular person. But it does provide the greatest amount of useable and useful truth that a sick person can handle at that particular moment.

In some illnesses one might need both the sick role and the "psych" role. A cancer patient might want to see a doctor for medical and surgical treatment and see a therapist to help not only with the emotional impact of the illness but the wear and tear of treatment, too. It is better that the therapist be unencumbered with Aesculapian authority so his full attention and energy can be devoted to the patient's psychological problems.

A different situation is encountered when psychological methods are used to treat cancer itself. Some therapists have been employing "guided imagery," a technique derived from Carl Jung. The patient is encouraged to make a mental image of the tumor and then to image some antagonist, such as a scavenger, which destroys it. There are claims that in this way some patients can rally their natural healing forces to contain or reverse the disease. We do not know at present whether this works, but we do know that patients who give up and turn their faces to the wall often die very quickly. Since guided imagery is one of those treatments which, in Claude Bernard's formulation,* cannot harm and may do good, and since it can and is being used with more conventional treatments, there seems every reason why those who want to use it should do so. Presumably, the treatment is limited to those who are good mental imagers.

However, one serious danger becomes visible when we understand the difference between the sick role and the "psych" role. Because it is not obviously a medical procedure, the patient receiving guided imagery may lose the sick

---

*The great French physiologist laid down the rules for experimental treatments in 1865 (Claude Bernard, *An Introduction to the Study of Experimental Medicine*). See Chapter XIV for a discussion of these rules.

role. If that happens, he or his family are liable to be blamed if the treatment fails or if there is some initial benefit and then the illness recurs. This has actually happened; in an article in the *Los Angeles Times*, Harry Nelson tells of a young Californian with cancer who was taught to image his brain turmor as consisting of hunks of Play-Doh. He then imaged himself seizing the Play-Doh and throwing it into a trash can. The tumor regressed, and the improvement in his skull could be seen on a brain scan. Unfortunately, not long after this the tumor started growing again and the boy died. The therapist proceeded to blame the parents for their son's death. He claimed, although admitting he could not prove it, that their divorce had caused the recurrence of the tumor. Even the most callous doctors usually do better than this.

As those who have attempted to assess the results of psychotherapy know, it is difficult to prove anything about the "psych" role *because it is holistic.* Scientific proof is only possible if one is willing to confine oneself to small and circumscribed aspects of phenomena, and according to some experts, it is further limited in that it can only proceed by generating refutable propositions, i.e., showing what is *not* true. Therapists do not operate within any such constraints, and it is difficult to prove when they have made a mistake. While responsible therapists are very cautious about making statements which cannot be proved, some, like the therapist mentioned, believe that holism means never having to say you're sorry.

If therapists are constrained neither by the rules governing scientific proof nor by the blame-free rules of the sick role, what *does* constrain them? At their best, therapists are constrained by the integrity of their relationship to the individual client and by their respect for the client's experience as reported by him. A good therapist never forces an interpretation on his client, but rather offers his best understanding of what his client is experiencing, the truth of which can only be confirmed by the client himself. Whether the client receives this high level of care depends very much on the personal qualities of the particular therapist. The "psych" role itself offers very little protection. While good therapy can be very good indeed, most therapy is not very good, and it is sometimes very bad. If the client progresses, all is well, but the "psych" role, unlike the sick role, is not built for failure and when failure occurs, it is almost inevitable that someone will be blamed.

The problem of explaining failure in the "psych" role is not a new one, and the rules were worked out a long time ago. In the *Malleus Malificarum*, an authoritative work on witchcraft first printed around 1486, Heinrich Kramer and James Sprenger have this to say about the failure of fifteenth-century psychotherapy, exorcism:

> For when a person is not healed, it is due either to a want of faith in the bystanders or in those who present the sick man, or to the sins of them who suffer from the bewitchment, or to a neglect of the due and fitting remedies, or to some flaw in the faith of the exorcist, or to the lack of a greater trust in the faith of another exorcist, or to the need of purgation and for the increased merit of the bewitched person.

The fifteenth-century authors of the *Malleus Malificarum* were explicit about the need to assign blame if the exorcism failed. The California therapist did not anticipate that his treatment might not work and was forced to improvise. What he came up with—blaming the boy's parents—was not an improvement of the performance of the proto-therapists of five hundred years ago. Therapists are likely to do less damage if they confine themselves to a respectful concern of their client's psychological experience and to disclaim any control over the outcome of major illnesses. Just as doctors are likely to become inflated when dealing with non-medical matters, so psychotherapists are similarly at risk in the dangerous but exhilarating atmosphere of clinical medicine.

When illnesses are poorly understood and treatments for

them are unsatisfactory, psychological explanations abound. This was true for general paresis and tuberculosis in the past and it is true for schizophrenia and cancer today. What usually happens is that as scientific explanations come into their own, everyone loses interest in the psychological aspects of the illness. In Thomas Mann's *The Magic Mountain*, psychoanalysis was offered as a treatment for tuberculosis, but what analyst today would feel it worthy of his interest to treat tubercular patients? Although many psychological correlates of this illness are known, our hopes for controlling it come from early detection and better medical treatment, not psychotherapy. We know of no illness that has been overcome by psychological knowledge.

In cultures where the scientific body of medical knowledge is small, medical treatments appear to be heavily psychological or "magical." This was not so noticeable in Dr. David Livingston's day when the treatments of European physicians were not that different from the medicine men, their African counterparts. Nevertheless, even cultures which are medically primitive, from our point of view, find it useful to distinguish the sick role from the "psych" role. Laura Bohannan's pills were not only accepted but demanded by her Nigerian tribesmen, but her advice on family and personal matters was considered worthless. The Tasaday, in spite of a total lack of medical tradition, eagerly accepted the help of the visiting doctors, but far from being able to offer them psychotherapy, we tried to learn how they manage to be so loving. In fact, it is unlikely that what they know about relationships is transferable to us because our culture is too different. The sick role is highly cross-cultural, the "psych" role is not.

The sick role and the "psych" role appear to be separate or at least separable, but what of body and mind? Our human organism does not come in two snap-together parts; it is a whole. But our experience of these two aspects is sufficiently different that we have two words to describe it. When we are at our best, we have no occasion to distinguish body from mind. A happy, healthy child playing around is a unified organism, but if he trips, falls, and cuts his knee, then he becomes aware of his body as separate from his mind. He will then need two kinds of treatment: medicine for the knee, comfort for the psyche.

It is the claim of some holistic healers that their treatments break down the distinction between body and mind. But is this really so? *All* medical treatments which work improve one's sense of well-being and thus improve the state of the mind. Treatments like guided imagery and biofeedback start with the mind and hope to effect changes in the body; again, the distinction is maintained. If body and mind were not separable, the phrases: "guided imagery causes tumors to regress" or "biofeedback reduces hypertension" would make no sense. Furthermore, the terms "tumor" and "hypertension" are derived from the diagnostic efforts of clinical (i.e., non-holistic) medicine. It is hard to see that they would have any meaning if one did not agree to a separation of body and mind. If there were a truly holistic treatment, it is not clear that one would be able to talk about it at all.

It is hardly news to doctors that relief from worry over illness or the resolution of an illness causes an easing of mental tensions and an improved state of mind. No one should underestimate the non-pharmacological aspects of ordinary medical care. There is the "psychic relief," as Dr. Max Pinner calls it, that comes with the conferral of the sick role and the knowledge that the doctor has taken the case and is willing to look after you. This is sometimes happily followed by actual relief from the illness itself—and there is probably no psychological relief greater than recovering one's health after an illness. The practice of medicine has never consisted solely of its physical and pharmacological effects.

But what about the effect of one's psychological state on the disease process? It seems reasonable to suppose that a good attitude—hopeful but not superstitious—would contribute toward one's chance of recovery. Being good to one's body—eating properly, getting rest, avoiding various poisons and pollutants—would seem prudent. Good sick-role behavior is very important, because it enlists the support of medical personnel and family and keeps up morale. Attitude is half the battle in *any* illness; if we did not believe that, there would be no point in writing this book!

A person who has a serious illness would do well to put his psychological house in order. The energy one would spend on family quarrels or old neurotic patterns is better spent on combating the illness. While it may be difficult to prove that psychological wholeness defeats any particular illness, it would seem worthwhile to rally all one's resources—physical, psychological, and spiritual—to cope with a threat to one's survival. If the battle goes badly and the illness cannot be defeated, then one will need one's entire resources to make a good end.

Valuable as the sick role is, it will not cover and is not meant to cover the entire range of human unhappiness and conflict. For this one is well advised to accept the "psych" role and try to find wise counsel for one's problems and needs. In fact, once a person has complained about being in difficulty, he is obliged to undertake either the sick role or the "psych" role, depending on which is appropriate. Sick? Call your doctor. Troubled? Call your therapist. Unless you live on a desert island or in a hermit's hut, your illness or unhappiness will affect the people around you, most especially your family. We do not have the right to moan and groan unless we are willing to take up the responsibilities of the sick role, the "psych" role, or both. The *swanelo* of family and social life demands it.

XIII *The Impaired Role*

OF THOSE WHO ENTER THE SICK ROLE, the most fortunate recover from their illnesses and resume their normal roles.
Others, like Ishi, leave the sick role for the dying role. Another possibility is that a person may recover from an illness
and yet be left with a permanent handicap or impairment.
This was the fate of a severely ill nineteen-month-old baby
named Helen Keller who went from the sick role to the impaired role, for her illness left her both deaf and blind. For
the rest of her life, she coped courageously with this appalling handicap and so became a famous and exemplary holder
of the impaired role.

The *swanelo* of the impaired role is quite different from
that of the sick role; this is made very clear in the slogan
"Hire the handicapped—it's good business." No one has
ever suggested it was good business to hire the sick! But the
handicapped are expected to make up for their impairment
by being exceptionally valuable in some other way. Impaired

people with great gifts, like Helen Keller and Franklin Roosevelt, are able to overcome their impaired status by exercising these gifts. Less talented impaired people try to maintain *swanelo* by being more reliable, more cheerful, less demanding on others—hence, it is good business to hire them.

In some cultures, impaired people earn their keep by providing a source of amusement for others. Laura Bohannan was horrified to find her informants doubled over with laughter when one of them told the story of yelling "Snake!" at blind Ngun. The point of the story, which she failed to grasp at first, was that a blind man would not know which way to jump because he could not see the snake. Recognizing that she was not amused, her informant explained he would not have played this trick if there really was a snake there. But this failed to mollify her; only when she went off to digest this unpleasant episode did she realize that "our kindness to the crippled and unfortunate is a luxury born of our ability to spare help and resources." Blind Ngun was fed and cared for; his contribution to the group's life was to provide some much-needed laughter. Playing tricks on the deaf, blind, and crippled was quite acceptable in Europe until about two hundred years ago. By our present standards, it is not an ideal arrangement, but we should not be surprised to learn that the *swanelo* of the impaired role is related to the resources, the sophistication, and the values of a particular culture.

In Helen Keller's America, the resources available to this doubly impaired child were enormous. A specially trained teacher, Miss Sullivan, was brought from the Perkins Institute for the Blind in Boston to devote herself entirely to the little Alabama girl. Helen was taken to the mountains and the seashore, to Niagara Falls, and to the Columbian Exposition in Chicago, where she toured the exhibits with her friend, Alexander Graham Bell. She graduated cum laude from Radcliffe College and wrote her autobiography in her sophomore year. Every possible educational and recreational experience was provided for her. Of course, not all deaf-blind children of her day were so fortunate; Helen came from a family which could afford such luxuries and knew enough to seek them.

Helen Keller's opportunities were great, but that alone would not have made her, as Mark Twain said, one of the two most interesting characters of the nineteenth century (the other being Napoleon). Helen was a brilliant and lovable person who constantly rewarded or, as we would say today, "reinforced" those who helped her, and in this way she inspired them to exert themselves further on her behalf. In *The Story of My Life*, her autobiography, she relates a letter she wrote in 1899 to William Wade, one of her many correspondents: "It gives me much pleasure to hear how much is being done for the deaf-blind. The more I hear of them, the more kindness I find. Why, only a little while ago people thought it quite impossible to teach the deaf-blind anything; but no sooner was it proved possible than hundreds of kind, sympathetic hearts were fired with the desire to help them, and now we see how many of these poor, unfortunate persons are being taught to see the beauty and reality of life. Love always finds its way into an imprisoned soul, and leads it out into the world of freedom and intelligence." Naturally, the recipients of these glowing letters responded by doing more and more for Helen and other deaf-blind people, and schools for the deaf-blind are still going strong today.

Helen Keller took an active part in the American Foundation for the Blind and traveled all over the world on its behalf. In the same way, Franklin Roosevelt was a major figure in the fight against poliomyelitis. It is not so easy for the retarded, another and much larger group of impaired people, to act on their own behalf or that of other retarded people. Nevertheless, it is not impossible. Nigel Hunt, a mongoloid (Down's syndrome) youth, wrote a diary, *The World of Nigel Hunt*, of which Dr. Lionel Penrose, in the foreword, said, "In consequence of a natural talent for verbal expression, which has been fostered by the devoted encouragement of his parents, Nigel has been able to give an account of the world as he sees it. He is thus, as it were, able to speak on behalf of thousands of similarly affected people who are either less gifted or have had less opportunity than he."

From Nigel's diary, we learn that he loves "pop" music, he enjoys traveling, and he makes friends wherever he goes. Like Helen Keller, he is a good "reinforcer"; when he was given some injections by a doctor while traveling in Europe, he said, "Danke schön, Herr Doktor," to which the doctor replied, "That's the first time I have ever been thanked." His parents view is that Nigel is a "precious soul in a somewhat handicapped body," and his father goes on to say, "We would not exchange him for the most brilliant child in the world and we have been richly and abundantly rewarded for all that we have tried to do for him."

A cheerful disposition, then, is a great asset in an impaired person; this quality goes a long way toward maintaining the *swanelo* of the relationship with those on whom they depend. In return, those caring for the impaired should do everything they can to make life pleasant for them. This is not necessarily true in the sick role, where medical treatments may be even more unpleasant than the disease itself and patients are at times expected to feel wretched and miserable. It may even be an ominous sign if a seriously ill person is too cheerful— he may not realize the seriousness of the illness; he may have decided he does not really need the treatment; he may, in fact, have slipped out of the sick role, and perhaps endangered his life in so doing. In the days before modern chemotherapy, the "false hope" of severe tuberculosis used to be seen as indicating a fatal outcome. It was a cause for fear, not rejoicing.

There is by definition no medical treatment for an impairment, so an impaired person does not have to endure the miseries and dangers which treatment so often entails. Rehabilitation, not treatment, is the key to a better life for the impaired. However, treatment and rehabilitation often can and have been confused. Fred Davis found in his study of polio victims and their families, *Passage Through Crisis: Polio Victims and Their Families,* that the families perceived the physiotherapists to be the most helpful and optimistic of the medical people, and they also believed physiotherapy was directed at curing the illness. In fact, the physiotherapists were not perceiving the children within the sick role—the doctors had already done all that could be done—but were trying to rehabilitate them, which is quite a different matter. In rehabilitation, even the tiniest improvements are a source of optimism, while in the sick role, a patient may improve one day and die the next. Davis felt that the physiotherapists would do well to help the family to distinguish between rehabilitation and cure so they could set more realistic goals from the start.

Coming to terms with a severe impairment is often a slow and painful business. Joni Eareckson, an athletic young woman, broke her neck in a diving accident and found herself in a hospital strapped to a Stryker frame, a sort of medical rack. Gradually she learned the degree of her impairment. After she had accepted the fact that she would never walk again, she still nursed the hope she would regain the use of her hands. When she was ready to leave a rehabilitation hospital for home, she asked her doctor whether she would ever use her hands again and he told her she would not. This was a severe blow to Joni. As she relates in her book:

I had accepted the fact that I'd never walk again. But I had believed I could still join the ranks of those handicapped persons who drive cars, make meals, work with their hands, and put their arms around someone they love. That I'd be able to drink a glass of water, bathe myself, brush my hair, and put on my own make-up. Little things, to be sure, but things important enough to make the difference between one who is merely handicapped and one who is totally dependent. Now, ever so slowly, the reality of my injury began to sink in—I was to be a quadriplegic *as long as I lived.*

Joni, understandably discouraged, felt she had nothing left and wanted to give up. But her friend Diana would have none of it, "Don't give me that. I saw people at Greenoaks and Rancho who were really bad off—blind, mute, deaf. Some even lost their minds—they were almost vegetables. *They* have nothing left, Joni. But you have your mind, your voice, your eyes, and your ears. You have everything you need. And you're going to make them work for you if I have anything to say." So Diana spoke for the morality of the impaired role: the impaired person who accepts the right to be cared for must undertake the reciprocal duties of the role, to use whatever he has in order to function.

One of Joni's therapists suggested she learn to use her mouth to do some of the things she would normally do with her hands. "No," was Joni's reply. "It's disgusting. Degrading. I won't do it!" The therapist did not press Joni on that occasion, but later Joni came to accept it. She not only learned to write a beautiful italic script with her mouth, but she also began to paint; she now has a career as an artist. She now occupies the impaired role in an exemplary way and so can be a source of hope and inspiration to others.

Stroke is a catastrophic illness followed by impairment. Without rehabilitation, the stroke victim may become immobile, speechless, depressed, apathetic. Yet vigorous rehabilitation may restore to varying degrees the person's normal functioning. Roald Dahl realized this, and when his wife, the actress Patricia Neal, came out of the hospital following a series of strokes, he immediately initiated a crash rehabilitation program. In Valerie Eaton Griffith's *A Stroke in the Family*, Dahl said, "Unless I was prepared to have a bad-tempered, desperately unhappy nitwit in the house, some very drastic action would have to be taken at once." Roald Dahl saw that it was not doctors he needed, but teams of amateur teachers. He phoned every neighbor and relative he could think of and soon had fifteen teachers working one-hour shifts. They worked with Pat to restore her ability to talk, read, write, and handle numbers; gradually she undertook the rest of her usual repertoire of skills and eventually resumed her career. Although each of her teachers protested that he or she knew nothing about helping a stroke victim, none needed any instruction once they had overcome their initial shyness about the job. They seemed to know instinctively what to do.

Patricia Neal herself was not at all certain she wanted to embark on this program. In an article in *Family Weekly*, she said, "Oh, what a mess I was. I wanted to give up. I was tired. I felt certain I was as good as I would ever be. But Roald, that slave-driving husband of mine, said no. And today I cannot thank him enough. That is why it is so important for a stroke victim to have someone around who cares enough to force him into doing whatever must be done, regardless of how cruel it may seem at the time. When a person has had a stroke, he doesn't feel like doing anything. I know from experience that had it been left up to me I would still be the idiot I was after that terrible ordeal in California." A huge rehabilitation center in Knoxville, Tennessee, has been named The Patricia Neal Rehabilitation Center. "Rehabilitation has come to be part of my name," she said.

Doctors rarely have much to do with impaired people, but a notable exception to this was Sir Frederick Treves, the same doctor who performed an appendectomy on Edward VII. In 1884, Dr. Treves noticed a sign on a shop near London Hospital announcing that, for twopence, one might see the "Elephant Man." Treves paid his twopence, and saw, according to Ashley Montague's *The Elephant Man*, "the most disgusting specimen of humanity I have ever seen." This grossly distorted creature was John Merrick, a twenty-one-year-old man who was so repulsive that his only method of earning a living was to exhibit himself as a freak. Worse, he was badly treated by the impresario who exhibited him. Treves, a lecturer in anatomy and surgery, gave Merrick his card and arranged to examine him at his hospital office. On the basis of this examination, Treves wrote a paper. Because Merrick's speech was almost unintelligible, Treves supposed him to be an imbecile. He did not expect to see Merrick again but he was wrong. Two years later, Treves was called by the police to see Merrick. Deserted by his exhibitors in Belgium, Merrick was given a ticket to Liverpool Street Station in London, and there Treves found him, huddled miserably in a corner, guarded by the police from the unkind and curious crowds. He had shown the police Treves's card, his only link with the civilized world. Treves took him by cab to London Hospital where he was given a bed and some food. Treves admitted this was a most irregular thing to do, for the hospital was neither a refuge nor a home for incurables. However, he got permission from the proper authorities, and soon Merrick was moved into a comfortable two-room apartment facing onto a courtyard. Money was raised in an appeal in the *Times*. So generous was the subscription, Merrick was provided for life without any charge on the hospital.

In his new environment, Merrick began to feel at home, and Treves soon learned that his guest was not only highly intelligent, but a man of great sensitivity, gentleness, and romantic temperament. It was then that Treves began his ingenious program of rehabilitation, which consisted of enlisting the help of well-bred ladies to come and visit Merrick and engage him in conversation—a program not unlike that devised by Roald Dahl for Patricia Neal. Merrick soon spent his days entertaining duchesses and countesses in his rooms. The height of his social career was a visit from Queen Alexandra, then Princess of Wales. Merrick said to Treves, "I am happy every hour of the day."

In 1890, Merrick was found dead in his bed, oddly enough because of his desire to sleep "like other people." His head was so heavy that he had to sleep propped up. On this one night he had tried to sleep with his head on a pillow, and the weight of it had broken his neck. He had borne so manfully so many aspects of his impairment, but he could not resist this one—and fatal—effort to be normal.

Treves was exceptional in his role with an impaired person, for Aesculapian authority does not normally cover impairment, only illness. How then do doctors fare when they themselves become impaired? We know they do poorly in the sick role, but from what we can learn, they do splendidly in the impaired role. Dr. Duncan Holbert, a California physician, is a polio victim and has been practicing medicine from an iron lung for more than twenty-five years. He has three attendants who care for him around the clock and are his hands and legs in the office. Dr. Holbert is an allergist, and he sees about sixty patients a day with the aid of his assistants. His patients sit on a bench in front of the lung so he can see them in his mirror. "Once you start talking to him, you don't realize that he's even in the lung," said one of his patients in an article in *Medical News*. He adapted so astonishingly well, he has been able to make his extremely severe impairment invisible, the hallmark of success in the impaired role. Evidently, while Aesculapian authority has a devastating effect on its holder in the sick role, there is no such conflict in the impaired role. If anything, Aesculapian authority helps blind patients to massive impairment.

The worst thing about an impairment is the lack of hope that it will ever change; the best thing is that its predictability allows the person to make a stable adjustment to his situation. However, life is full of surprises, and an impairment may quite suddenly turn into something else. An article in the London *Times* on May 31, 1975 tells of Mr. Jon Lawrence, a forty-three-year-old blind man living in England, who tripped over his Seeing Eye dog, fell down a flight of stairs, struck his head, and recovered his sight! He had been blind for four years. The fact that he had a guide dog shows he believed his condition to be permanent and had settled down to live with it as best he could.

Ms. Henrietta Hepler, of Lead, South Dakota, had resigned herself to a life of being bent double; she was told she had rheumatoid arthritis and would just have to live with it. However, in June 1974, she got a new diagnosis, ankylosing spondylitis, and for this condition, an operation—albeit a risky one—was possible. She was motivated to take the risk because her impairment was getting worse. It was no longer possible to perceive herself as someone who made a stable adjustment to an unchanging impairment. She now saw herself as someone with an illness which would inevitably get worse unless she did something about it. She took the chance and got her reward: she is now able to stand straight and sleep in a flat position. The opening sentence of the newspaper article "Woman Risks Life to Stand Straight—A spunky 41-year-old woman gambled her life for the chance of standing up straight—and won."—shows that social approval is available for someone who abandons the impaired role (under medical advice, of course) to the more dangerous but hopeful sick role. Had the situation been the other way around and Ms. Hepler had switched from the sick role to the impaired role, there would have been no newspaper article. In order to make news then, she would have had to overcome her impairment in some especially ingenious or courageous way.

Both the sick role and the impaired role are legitimate ways of organizing certain kinds of human misfortune. Both roles are familiar to us; we are all sick from time to time and most of us accumulate at least minor impairments as we grow older: losses in eyesight, hearing, stamina, etc. But since the two roles require such different behavior and have such different consequences, it is well worth our while to ask in every case whether the particular person is in the role which best suits his needs.

XIV *The Guinea Pig Role*

THE GUINEA PIG is a small, charming, defenseless animal that has come to be the symbol of experimental medicine. When human beings take part in an experiment, we sometimes speak of them as human guinea pigs. We need to distinguish between experiments which go on within the sick role and those which go on in what we shall call the guinea-pig role because, depending upon the role, the rules are quite different.

Within the sick role, experimentation goes on all the time. Almost any medical treatment is experimental in some sense: either a standard treatment is being given to someone who has some other disease as well or a patient takes a medicine in a fashion not envisioned by his doctor (suppositories have been known to be taken by mouth) or the preparation is made by some other drug company than that usually given and has somewhat different properties. Even more important is the wide range of personal idiosyncrasy which adds to the experimental nature of all treatments. The wide and probably growing variability of human beings, due to successful medical treatment and prevention, makes us quite unlike the carefully interbred, standardized laboratory animals. While human beings are becoming increasingly variable, laboratory animals are becoming increasingly standardized. In fact, it is difficult to give the same patient the same treatment. For every treatment, however trivial, changes, perhaps only to a small extent, the biology, pharmacology, and immunology of the patient. Most of these natural experiments pass unnoticed or, if noticed, are of no particular importance, but from time to time an astute doctor or patient learns something important from them and improves the treatment as well as advancing medical knowledge.

There are many kinds of experimentation in clinical practice: accidental changes in treatment, natural experiments from which something is learned, planned clinical trials for improving a particular patient's chances of recovery, and new and perhaps dangerous experiments which are undertaken because the patient's life hangs in the balance and no known treatment works. In all these treatments, *the role does not change:* the patient is still in the sick role and the doctor is still exercising his Aesculapian authority to benefit that patient by applying such medical knowledge as is available at that time and place. The goal is to do for each patient as much good and as little harm as possible. Doctors and patients vary in how adventurous they are, how imaginative in coming up with new treatment possibilities. A cautious doctor-patient pair might cling to well-known but unsuccessful treatments, while in the next office a more adventurous medical dyad might be trying out a whole series of new drugs to discover whether any of them work. The degree of success depends on the astuteness of the doctor and patient, the medical knowledge available, the nature and severity of the illness, and luck—or, as some would say, the patient's fate or God's will. There are many unknowns in the treatment of an illness, but the one thing that can be known with absolute certainty is whether or not the patient is in the sick role.

For those within the protection of the sick role, the rules are fairly clear; they were laid down more than a century ago by the great physiologist Claude Bernard in his work *An Introduction to the Study of Experimental Medicine*, "It is our duty and our right to perform an experiment on man when it can save his life, cure him, or gain him some personal benefit." He also said, "among the experiments that may be tried on man, those that can only harm are forbidden, those that are innocent are permissible, and those that may do good are obligatory." Clinical or therapeutic experiments such as those covered by Bernard's rules are inextricably bound up with the sick role. Their purpose is the betterment of a particular patient by the person treating him, most often his doctor, but sometimes the patient himself.

We have an account of a young woman who conducted a very successful clinical experiment on herself, but then unfortunately put herself into the hands of a doctor who did not subscribe to Claude Bernard's rules. This young woman, whose mother had coeliac disease, suspected that she, too, might be allergic to gluten and experimentally put herself on a gluten-free diet. She was delighted with the results and would have let well enough alone except she was a bit too medically pious to do without an "official" diagnosis. In her uncertainty, she felt she could not refuse foods containing gluten when dining with friends; she also worried that if she were ever hospitalized she would not be allowed a gluten-free diet. So, in pursuit of medical legitimation, she went to a specialist recommended by her family doctor. To her horror, she discovered that the report of her successful experiment was not enough to convince this man of science: he wanted to have her small intestine biopsied, which required that she return to eating gluten for a period before the test. She reluctantly agreed, spent a miserably sick Christmas, had the biopsy, and was then *officially* put on a gluten-free diet. She knew there was something wrong with this second experiment, but she could not put her finger on it.

The young woman's self-experiment was well within Claude Bernard's rules: it could and did help and it could do no harm. It was quite otherwise with the specialist. In addition to making her sick beforehand, the biopsy, which was done under general anesthetic, carried a small but quite definite risk. The benefits *to her* could not possibly have been greater than the benefits of not eating gluten, which she was already doing. What then was the purpose of the second experiment? It certainly did not fall under the general medical ruling of *nil nisi bonum* (nothing unless good); she was made sick and could have died. What the specialist wanted was "proof." He was acting as a scientist whose goal is the truth not as a clinician whose goal is the betterment of the particular patient in his charge. Unknown to herself and without being warned by her doctor of this change in role, the young woman had become the subject—or victim—of a rather pedestrian scientific investigation. She had consented to be a patient; she had unwittingly become a guinea pig.

Claude Bernard's rules cover any treatment no matter how "far-out," provided the person is in the sick role. If the treatment cannot harm and can help, it is obligatory to try it. Doctors who are not familiar with these rules may be unnecessarily conservative in their treatment, thus driving patients who are more adventurous or more desperate into the arms of "far-out" practitioners, some of whom are merely unorthodox and others who are quacks or charlatans. Doctors understandably get very upset when they learn their former patients have left the fold, so to speak. But orthodox medicine does not have all the answers and never will, so doctors must resign themselves to having competitors. Their best course of action is to be experimental within the meaning of Claude Bernard's rules so that they do not lose patients whom they might be able to help.

There is a legitimate guinea-pig role, but it is not the same as the sick role and is not covered by Claude Bernard's rules. In its purest form, a healthy person volunteers to be part of a scientific experiment, the purpose of which is to find out something new which cannot be discovered in any other way. The investigator advertises his proposed experiment—emphasizing its scientific, aesthetic, and ethical virtues—and hopes to find people who will join him in his adventure into the unknown. His position is not very different from that of a leader of a zoological, anthropological, or archeological expedition into the wilderness: he must convey, to the best of his knowledge, the risks of the expedition and at the same time hope the excitement and possible fame of the expedition will lure adventurous types into joining him. If there is any payment involved, it is usually of a token sort and not sufficient to constitute the sole reason for joining a risky but exciting undertaking.* While many of us will not risk life and limb in this fashion, there are quite a few individuals for whom life is never quite dangerous enough, and there is no great difficulty in locating them, provided that the possible risks and benefits are made sufficiently clear.

If an experimental subject loses interest in a once-exciting experiment, there is little the investigator can do about it. This occurred in the famous case of the army surgeon, Dr. William Beaumont, and the young trapper, Alexis St. Martin. After having Dr. Beaumont peering into the hole in his stomach on and off for eleven years, St. Martin had had enough. Although Dr. Beaumont was as enthusiastic as ever about his unique guinea pig, St. Martin, now married and with a family, could not be persuaded to resume the experiments. Beaumont wrote letters to St. Martin pleading, coaxing, promising, and cajoling, and he was not above trying to make St. Martin feel guilty about all that had been done for him. But Beaumont never tried to deceive or coerce. Carl Wiggers, writ-

* The young lady whose small intestine was biopsied presumably paid the doctor-investigator; she was a *paying* guinea pig.

ing of Beaumont's high ethical standards as an experimenter,* believed that Beaumont could have exerted certain prerogatives of his military status or could have compelled St. Martin to remain with him by refusing financial aid for St. Martin's return home. Today, an unscrupulous experimenter with a unique subject might be tempted to disguise the experiments as treatments, persuading the subject that the "treatments" were in his own interest. But Beaumont did none of these things; reluctantly, he brought the experiments to an end.

Another class of volunteer guinea pigs consists of people who either have an illness which has not yielded to existing treatments or people who are at risk of getting some illness unless protected against it. A man named Floyd Miller, who suffered from Parkinson's disease, met Dr. George Cotzias at a restaurant dinner party. Dr. Cotzias had pioneered the use of L-dopa, the drug Mr. Miller was using to control his illness. Mr. Miller told the doctor about the course of his illness. According to a *Reader's Digest* article Dr. Cotzias proposed that Mr. Miller join a research effort of which he was the chief, "We have compounded a new drug which we are experimenting with. . . . It might help you, but to receive it you would have to volunteer for our research program. You would be hospitalized for at least a month, perhaps longer, and after discharge you would be an out-patient for the rest of your life. We might not help you. You might even get worse. But you would be making an important contribution to the battle against Parkinson's." "How soon can you take me?" was Mr. Miller's response.

At one point in the hospitalization, Mr. Miller made some suggestions about altering the dosage of his medication. When Dr. Cotzias did not respond favorably to these suggestions Mr. Miller said, airily, "I can always try my own experiments with dosage when I return home." Now patients who are only in the sick role very often make such experiments

* "Human Experimentation as Exemplified by the Career of Dr. William Beaumont."

with dosage, sometimes with the knowledge and agreement of their doctor and sometimes not. However, having agreed to be part of a formal experiment the chief purpose of which was to gain further knowledge of Parkinson's disease, Mr. Miller did not have that right, and Dr. Cotzias spelled out the duties of the research subject in no uncertain terms, "You are part of a research team that includes not only the people in this room, not only the scientists and nurses and aides in this building, but several hundred brave men and women who have occupied these beds before you. Not a single one of them has ever arbitrarily broken a protocol pertaining to a drug we asked him to take. . . . If you fail to follow orders, your records can distort and falsify our ultimate findings. If I ever discover you doing this, I'll throw you out of the program." So speaks the scientific investigator to his research subject. The clinical doctor speaking to his patient would have no occasion to invoke hundreds of other people; he speaks only of two people, himself and his patient.

When discussions arise about the "necessity" of using mentally retarded children or adults, prisoners, or other captive populations for experimental purposes, it is often assumed that it is impossible to get real volunteers. But reputable and imaginative investigators do not seem to have this difficulty. Dr. Cotzias said, "Never once have I asked a patient to take a new, potentially dangerous drug and have him refuse. They might hesitate, they might say, 'Let me think it over,' but they always end by saying 'yes.' " The physician-investigators described by Renee Fox in *Experiment Perilous* were able to inspire the patients in their metabolic unit with the desire to participate in new medical and surgical treatments. Many of these patients were dying, and offering themselves as experimental subjects was one of the few ways they could make their last days meaningful. For some people, dying as a martyr to science may provide a more heroic end than simply losing to a disease. What the volunteers Fox described had in common was that they were truly volunteers;

while they were captives of their illness, they were not captives of their doctors.

We would argue that no *child* can be a volunteer. As Paul Ramsey put it in *The Patient as Person*, "No child or adult incompetent can choose to become a participating member of medical undertakings, and no one else on earth should decide to subject these people to investigations having no relation to their own treatment. That is a canon of loyalty to them. This they claim of us simply by being a human child or incompetent. When he is grown, a child may put away childish things and become a true volunteer. This is the meaning of being a volunteer: that a man enter and establish a consensual relation in some joint venture for medical progress." A. Herbert Schwartz, in an article in *The New England Journal of Medicine,* showed that of a group of children hospitalized for research testing, those under the age of eleven did not understand that their hospitalization was for research rather than treatment, in spite of careful preparation. Of those over eleven, the five out of six who did understand showed overwhelming anxiety.

Ramsey cites one exception to the rule against submitting children to medical investigation: when there are epidemic conditions which endanger the individual child. In the case of the polio vaccine trials, the parents had to weigh the risk of the new vaccine against the risk of the child getting polio that summer. As for using prisoners as volunteers, Ramsey argues that it is not impossible and might be desirable, but it is very difficult to guarantee a truly non-coercive situation.

If we must lean over backwards to ensure that no one becomes an experimental subject without fully informed consent, the case is quite otherwise within the sick role. There are stories in circulation in which a surgeon tells a patient exactly and in the most exquisite detail what will or might happen to him during an operation. The patient is so frightened he refuses the operation and later sues the surgeon for mental anguish. We suspect these stories are mythical, that they reflect the fear that patients will be treated as if they are experimental subjects. The patients in these tales are fully justified in their wrath; they have asked for the bread of Aesculapian authority and have been given the stone of scientific information. While patients must not be shanghaied into operations and while they have a right to know what courses of action are open to them, they also have a right not to be given information which is of no particular use to them at the moment. One can be honest and honorable without inflicting on the patient every horrific possibility. If in doubt, the patient has the right to ask for a second opinion, and the good surgeon or physician encourages rather than opposes such prudence. What the patient needs is a clear, simple description of the options open to him or her, plus an expert opinion as to which moves would be best in the particular circumstances.

For most of us, the danger of being coerced into a medical experiment is far less probable than the danger of being mistakenly treated as an experimental subject by a clinical doctor instead of as a patient. The number and complexity (and cost) of laboratory tests and the publicity about double-blind clinical trials has led many to imagine that both diagnosis and treatment are far more objective and exact than they really are. Medicine is still a craft, not an applied science. The person who believes there are exact answers to every medical question will be disappointed, and the doctor who believes it will practice poor medicine. A doctor today may tell a patient, after a battery of tests proves negative, that there is nothing wrong with him; worse still, he may tell the patient "It's all in your head." What he means is he does not know what is wrong with the patient and the existing tests have not helped him to make a diagnosis. *A test is not a diagnosis!* The most a test can do is provide the doctor with some useful information. If a test is positive, it may indicate the patient has a particular condition. But if a test is negative, it does not necessarily mean the patient does not have that or some other condition; it only means the test has not proved useful in that case.

Another trap for the unwary patient is the use of the word placebo. The term originated within clinical medicine and came to mean a harmless, inexpensive, and, perhaps, inactive pill that would give the patient the feeling something was being done for him when, for one reason or another, very little could be done. Sometimes it was given because the patient was dying, sometimes because the doctor didn't know what was wrong and there was no treatment for the illness, and sometimes because the patient was upset rather than ill and needed reassurances. The placebo was Aesculapian authority made tangible, and when properly used, it remains just that. Dr. Will Pickles found that unless he prescribed some medicine for his country patients, he could not collect his fee!

Some people feel better after being given a chemically inactive substance, and this is called the placebo effect. With the rise of experimental medicine, it was thought essential to eliminate the placebo effect when testing new drugs in order to prove the drug was doing what it was supposed to be doing. While this seems a reasonable thing to do, it is fraught with unanticipated and indeed unrecognized technical and ethical difficulties. If a patient is unknowingly given a placebo (and it would have to be unknown to *be* a placebo) because his doctor has agreed to test some new drug rather than to treat his patient, then the very basis of the doctor-patient relationship has been undermined. The trust which the patient must feel in order to place himself in the hands of the doctor has been violated. Surely no one would return to a doctor after learning that instead of being treated for his illness, he was being used as a guinea pig.

It has become fashionable to try out new drugs on large populations of hospitalized or institutionalized patients, especially the mentally ill or the mentally retarded, with so-called double-blind experiments—half the population is given the new drug, half is given a placebo, and *no one* knows who's getting which. This makes sense if the drug might benefit and cannot harm those patients and if its efficacy is not known and cannot be known in any other way. However, if the drug is already known to have some benefit, it is unethical to withhold it from half the population, who would then go on suffering from the illness while believing that they are being treated. Another difficulty with these studies is that it is assumed the double-blind can be maintained; however, most drugs have side effects and it does not take the nurses (who actually administer the drugs) or the patients very long to determine which is which. Double-blind experiments are therefore frequently not blind.*

A further difficulty is that in order to preserve the double blind, it is usual to give every patient the same dose of the drug. The more individual variation in the treatment, the more easily the patient will realize he is or is not getting the active treatment. When a standard dose is used it is likely to be active for most patients in any particular sample, but it may well be too little for some of them or too much for others. Patients are therefore being exposed to two different kinds of dangers by employing the double-blind technique: some biases are eliminated, but others are introduced. Had Dr. Cotzias given the same dose of the new drug, Sinemet, to each of his experimental subjects, perhaps only a few, perhaps none, would have responded to that particular dose, whereas many or even all of them might have responded to a dosage adjusted to their individual needs. Double-blind studies, then, thought by some to be the hallmark of scientific medicine, may be poor science as well as poor medicine.

Because of the publicity given to double-blind experiments, many clinical doctors now feel they must constantly be on the look-out for patients claiming to feel better on some simple, unorthodox, or self-prescribed treatment when

---

* Blumenthal, Burke, and Shapiro, "The Validity of 'Identical Matching Placebos.' "

they are "really" just getting a placebo effect. This was the view of the specialist treating the young woman with the gluten allergy. What reason had he to doubt her story except for the fear that she was only getting a placebo effect? The fact that she became ill again when returned to a gluten diet should have been proof enough that the effect was real; the biopsy was totally unnecessary. When a schizophrenic patient, who had been treated with psychotherapy at one clinic for twenty years, reported to his latest psychiatrist that he had been taking megavitamins and was now beginning to feel somewhat better, the doctor said, "Oh, that's just a placebo effect." The patient roared, "Then *you* give me a placebo effect—I've been coming here for twenty years!" Both these doctors turned their backs on self-experiments which could do no harm and which could (and did) do good, a type of experiment Claude Bernard said was not only permissible but obligatory.

A practicing doctor who wants to be as scientific as possible without exchanging the doctor-patient relationship for the investigator-subject relationship would do well to emulate that greatest of scientific practitioners, Sherlock Holmes. Conan Doyle is supposed to have based the character of Holmes on his teacher, Dr. Joseph Bell. In Vincent Starett's *The Private Life of Sherlock Holmes*, Bell is reported to have said, "From close observation and deduction, gentlemen, it is possible to make a diagnosis that will be correct in any case. However, you must not neglect to ratify your deductions, to substantiate your diagnoses, with the stethoscope and by all other recognized and everyday methods." What Bell failed to note, possibly because he took it completely for granted, was that only an open-minded and imaginative look at the data will yield deductions and diagnoses *worth* ratifying and substantiating. As Peter Medawar, in *Induction and Intuition in Scientific Thought*, put it, "Scientific reasoning is an exploratory dialogue that can always be resolved into two voices, or two episodes of thought, imaginative and critical, which alternate and interact." The good scientist, the good physician, and the good detective go back and forth between what Medawar has called "the possible and the actual." In earlier times, physicians tended to err in the direction of being too imaginative and too uncritical; now the shoe is on the other foot, and we must beware of physicians who are too critical and too unimaginative, like the Scotland Yard detectives whom Holmes so often outdid.

The sophisticated patient must make sure he does not become a guinea pig unless he and his doctor agree that they both wish to enter this new and different relationship. On the other hand, the patient wants to make sure his doctor is sufficiently imaginative to undertake clinical experiments in the manner advocated by Claude Bernard. It is a poor doctor who will try new treatments even if they cannot help and might harm his patient; it is an equally poor doctor who will not try any new treatment even if it can only help and will not harm the patient. What we all want—and will get, if we know enough to assert ourselves—is a physician both imaginative and critical, open to what is possible but constricted by what is actual. The sophisticated patient does not need to be coerced into the guinea-pig role; he can decide for himself whether he wants it or not. He will not be a passive and ignorant occupant of the sick role, but a responsible and fully participating member of the doctor-patient dyad.

XV *The Dying Role*

THOSE WHO ARE ADMITTED to the sick role cannot leave by the same door through which they entered. Time does not flow backwards, and however favorable the outcome of their illness they will never be quite the same again. Those who recover return to their normal roles; their illness becomes part of their personal history, stored in the vaults of memory. The impaired relinquish the sick role for the impaired role. But what of those who, inspite of the best efforts of medicine, are not going to recover? The role which offers them the most protection, solace, and dignity, the role of choice, is the dying role.

The dying role is very different from the sick role. Only a person in the sick role can properly accept medical treatment. The sick person puts up with the risks and miseries of medical treatment in the hope it may restore function or prolong life. Once it has been determined that no further efforts will reverse the dying process, medical treatment is no longer in order. The dying person—no longer a patient—has a right to such comforts and easements as medicine allows, but he has neither the right to demand nor the duty to accept medical treatment. A fourteen-year-old Illinois girl named Heidi Biggs was found to have a rare form of cancer known to be incurable. Heidi, her family, and her doctors all agreed that she was dying, and so medical treatment was not appropriate. Instead, every effort was made to honor the dying girl's wishes. What Heidi wanted was to see Hawaii before she died and if possible to go horseback riding there. Mr. Russell Penny, a Canadian who had heard about Heidi, raised funds to pay for the trip. When Heidi and her mother arrived in Hawaii, they were greeted by floral leis and a cake inscribed: "Heidi, enjoy your trip." The trip was the last indulgence it was possible to give her, for she died as she reached home.

This story—told in *The Birmingham News* of February 17, 1975—shows quite clearly the difference between the sick role and the dying role. Had her doctors considered her treatable, they would have exerted great pressure upon Heidi and upon the family for her to come into the hospital and be treated. They would have been angry and indignant had she taken a vacation in Hawaii instead. If she had had appendicitis instead of a rare cancer and had announced that she intended to go horseback riding in Hawaii instead of coming into the hospital, she would have elicited frowns and head-shakings at her irresponsible behavior. But once a person has been installed in the dying role, all sorts of indulgences, like the condemned prisoner's last meal, are countenanced. And the greatest indulgence is the right to refuse further treatment.

In earlier days, it was not the final vacation but the final disposition of the soul which became the main consideration when one was installed in the dying role. In Boswell's biography, *The Life of Samuel Johnson,* Johnson asked his doctor to tell him plainly whether he thought he, Johnson, could recover. The doctor first inquired whether Johnson thought he could bear the whole truth, whatever it might be. Johnson said he could, and so the doctor told him he could not recover without a miracle. Johnson said, "Then, I will take no more physick, not even my opiates, for I have prayed that I may render up my soul to God unclouded."

Where the patient, the family, and the doctor are in agreement, it is possible to make a smooth transition from the sick role to the dying role. But this agreement does not always occur, and the possibility of confusion grows with technical advances in medicine. A Florida hospital recently sued a twenty-one-year-old girl, Ronda Seaman, and her family, for trespass. In this case, the girl had been in a deep coma for more than a year. According to a *Los Angeles Times* article, the hospital administrator argued that the hospital was intended for the care of acutely ill patients and Ronda showed "virtually no possibility of recovery or significant improvement." He wished her transferred to a nursing home, although it seemed likely she would die if such a move were undertaken. Her father, Irwin Seaman, contended that his daughter was fighting for her life, and "when someone fights for her life, she needs every edge she can get." Ronda's mother, Adele Seaman, claimed she could see improvement in Ronda, "At first, her eyes were closed all the time. Now, she opens them during the day and closes them at night." In this dispute, the hospital claimed Ronda was beyond medical help and they had a right to stop treating her, while her family claimed she was still in the sick role and had the right to "every edge she can get."

Exactly the opposite claim was made in the more famous case of Karen Ann Quinlan, told by her parents in *Karen Ann: The Quinlans Tell Their Story*. Here it was the family who placed their daughter in the dying role, while the doctors and the hospital continued to perceive her as being in the sick role. This twenty-one-year-old New Jersey woman went into a coma of unknown origin in April 1975. At first, the family and the doctors were in agreement that everything possible should be done to save Karen's life. Then, as Karen's condition deteriorated, the doctors were no longer able to hold out the hope she would recover. When all the Quinlans had accepted this prognosis, they went to Gates of Heaven Cemetery and purchased a family plot, thus demonstrating they understood that one of their family was going to die. They then requested that the doctor and the hospital honor the Catholic church's teachings on these matters: that "extraordinary means" need not be used to sustain the life of a hopeless case. At this point, however, the very doctor whose gloomy prognosis had persuaded them that Karen Ann was dying suddenly balked; he refused to stop treating Karen in the intensive care unit where she had now been for ten months. In response to the request that he discontinue the use of a respirator, he said, "I find that I will not do it." Karen was still his "patient."

The Quinlans were then in an awkward spot. Since they were no longer in agreement with their doctor, they ought to have dismissed him and found another. Many other doctors had expressed the opinion that the Quinlan's view—that Karen was in the dying role, not the sick role—was correct. However, the Quinlans were extremely medically pious and were not accustomed to standing their ground with doctors. The case went to the courts, and when it reached the Supreme Court of New Jersey, the judges wanted to know whether the Quinlans had asked the doctors to "get off the case." The Quinlans had not, because they evidently did not know this was their right, nor did they know how to dismiss a doctor.

The court supported the Quinlans' request, but even with this reassurance, their doctor continued to regard Karen as his "patient." The situation was resolved when it was found possible to wean Karen off the respirator and thus move her out of the intensive care unit. The same doctor who had clung to treating her now abruptly lost interest in her, claiming she was now a "chronic care" (i.e., dying) patient and the hospital had no facilities or nurses for that kind of patient! She was safely moved to a nursing home, where she is now, being cared for (but not treated) as she slowly fades away.

This case inspired horror in many people because it shows that if one's doctor is unwilling or unable to facilitate the transition from the sick role to the dying role, one might be marooned for a very long time in a role-less limbo. Karen hooked up to machines in an intensive care unit was not in the sick role—for nothing that was done for her could possibly help her to recover—nor was she in the dying role—for the dying person belongs to himself and his family, not to medicine. Once Karen was moved to the nursing home, the horror went out of the case because she was no longer subjected to the rigors of medical treatment. It was then possible for the family to exercise its rights to personal care for Karen. Karen's mother said she was going to buy some pretty nightgowns for Karen and split them up the back and hem them. She said to her husband, "I can finally do something for her with my own hands, Joe, for the first time in a year."

Medicine has gradually usurped the dying role, but this has occurred mainly by default. Doctors would gladly get rid of this unwanted responsibility if they knew how. It has never been a major part of the doctor's role to minister to the dying. Rather, it was his role to signal that the last act of the play was about to begin and if possible to prepare the patient and the family for this event. He sometimes gave a placebo which enabled him to maintain a symbolic presence while withdrawing his no-longer-needed technical help. Then the other actors were ushered in: the family and friends of the dying person, representatives of the law, religion, philosophy, or ethics.

One sees such a death in Evelyn Waugh's novel, *Brideshead Revisited*. Lord Marchmain, abroad for many years, comes home at last to die at Brideshead. Because he is an important man, a peer of the realm, a man of wealth and property, the father of four adult children, and a lapsed Catholic, there are a great many complex arrangements that have to be made during his final days. Lord Marchmain does not take up his old rooms, but orders his belongings put in the Chinese drawing room, where he will sleep in the "Queen's bed," with its velvet cornice and twisted gilt columns. Into this museum of a room, his Italian mistress, his children, the doctor, the nurses, the servants, the solicitors, and a priest come and go, trying to meet his wishes, pressing their claims, trying to judge how close to death he is, wanting to bring it all to that successful conclusion, a good death. The doctor is pressed for his opinion about whether the dying patient, who has already ejected the priest once, should be allowed to see him again. To this the doctor replies, "My business is with the body. It's not my business to argue whether people are better alive or dead, or what happens to them after death. I only try to keep them alive." The priest proves, not surprisingly, much more comfortable about his role with the dying man and predicts correctly that the early rebuff meant little, that all will go well at the end. When Lord Marchmain crosses himself at last, the priest says, "Well, now, and that was a beautiful thing to see. I've known it to happen that way again and again." And so Lord Marchmain dies with his religious, legal, and family affairs in order.

Central to Lord Marchmain's acquisition of the dying role was the Chinese drawing room, a room on the ground floor which was easily accessible and large enough to hold all the people who helped him to accomplish the transition from this world to the next. By contrast, Elizabeth Kubler-Ross had to ask for two chairs for the parents of a dying leukemic girl. In an article in the *New York Times* she said, "I cannot comprehend why patients have to die in an intensive care unit and their families sit alone outside in a waiting room. I was told the mother cannot get a chair because she stayed more than five minutes last time." Now the intensive care unit is, spatially, at the very core of the hospital's most strenuous efforts to rescue a sick person from death. It is not surprising that there is no room for visitors, anymore than there would be in an operating room. If the girl is fighting for her life, then she must forego visits from her family during that time, and her family must agree to stay out of the way while the hospital staff try to save her. However, if she is in the dying role, then she and her family have the right to meet death as they see fit, while the hospital staff have the duty to stay out of the way and to give their final ministrations as unobtrusively as possible.

The gradual disintegration of the dying role seems to be closely related to its change in location from home to hospital during the last seventy-five to one hundred years. Building vast techno-palaces for doctors is a very recent occupation. Earlier eras had splendid palaces for priests, for gods, for religious orders, for holy relics, for kings and queens and those aspiring to be such, but not for doctors. Hospitals run by religious orders gave at least as much attention to the soul of their patients as to their bodies. The modern, secular hospital reflects the decline of religious authority and the relative rise in Aesculapian authority; it contributes to that decline by providing no appropriate space where the clergy, the family, and the patient can come together at the time of the patient's impending death. Hospital architecture reflects what is now held to be important and possible: saving lives at all costs. And so, in the modern hospital, the sick role has squeezed out the dying role both socially and spatially.

If doctors do not acknowledge the existence of the dying role, they block the patient's exit from the sick role. Instead of being allowed to enter the dying role and gain its comforts, the dying person may still be perceived as a patient—a *failed* patient. The failed patient is a reproach to medicine, and so the doctor feels he must undertake more and more drastic measures even though he knows rationally that nothing he does will alter the outcome. One of the ironies of this situation is that the more skillful and devoted the doctor and the more deeply he cares about the patient, the more difficult it will be for him to give up the fight. Nature abhors a vacuum, so the doctor who is not aware of the dying role is loath to let his patient out of the sick role.

This was the case with young Eric Lund, who, with the aid of his doctors and nurses, put up a splendid four-and-a-half-year battle against leukemia. Eric had so many remissions and relapses that it was difficult to know when the game was up. During his third remission he made a trip across country with a friend in an old van—using money he had earned working part-time at a funeral home while on passes from Memorial Hospital! At one point, it seemed almost certain that he would die: he developed an infection, his temperature went up to 106, and despite blood transfusions from forty to fifty people a day, his platelet count remained zero. A newspaper man who was a friend of the family put a story, "Soccer Star Battles Leukemia," in the Lund's hometown paper which brought soccer players, the entire lacrosse team, and other friends from the University of Connecticut to the Donor Room at Memorial Hospital. The nurses who knew Eric came running to his room after they finished their duty in other parts of the hospital to help bring him back to life, "Eric! Can you hear me?" "Eric! Come on, love!" In her book *Eric*, Doris Lund recalled, "Barbara. Maureen. Little Cathy, after eight-hour duty on another floor in Memorial. This was not nursing, it was something way beyond. A human being was going over the edge; other human beings were trying to pull him back. With all its ugliness, I felt the beauty of life that night, the beauty of people working together. Everything suddenly seemed part of the whole. Help was forever on the way. For a moment it was as if all the good in the world were known to me and held inside my head." The Lunds later learned that the top doctors had agreed that Eric would surely die that weekend. But they never stopped fighting for his life; they fought for it minute by minute.

The doctors and nurses were at their very best in Eric's

critical illness, even though they all knew they would soon lose him to leukemia. The time they bought for him allowed him almost a year of love with a beautiful nurse, MaryLou. He was able to bring her home for a visit and to take her on a final Christmas trip. They returned in time for Eric to throw a final, epic New Year's Eve party which lasted for four days, the "bash of the century." Then Eric went into the hospital to die. He asked his mother whether his younger sister was "ready." He gave MaryLou a copy of Elizabeth Kubler-Ross's book, *On Death and Dying*. He told his mother, "Walk in the world for me. . . ." He asked MaryLou, "Can I rest now? I'm so tired. Is it all right to rest now?"

Then Eric's kidneys failed. The doctors called the family together to confer about a possible operation. Dr. Dowling, who had fought so hard to save Eric, now explained to the family that although he wanted to know how each of them felt about an operation, he would have to make the decision. Doris Lund and MaryLou, the two people most closely attuned to Eric's feelings, felt that although his spirit was unbroken, his body could take no more. Doris Lund said, "I think we've come to the end. Eric wants to rest. I say let him go. . . ." Nevertheless, Dr. Dowling decided to operate on Eric.

Eric survived the operation but did not regain consciousness. MaryLou warned the family that if he went into cardiac arrest, a Code Alert would be sent out and all the interns would come running to pound on his chest and get his heart started again. MaryLou said to Eric's nurses, "Let him die with dignity. . . . I promised him it would be peaceful." The nurses agreed to stand in the doorway and fight off the Code Alert! Here one sees the hospital at its most bizarre, unable to stop its frenzied life-saving activities, so splendidly appropriate a year before, but now futile, pointless, and even cruel.

Eric lay dying in a room with an intern and a nurse quietly

checking dials, needles, and charts. The room belonged to the family now, Doris taking leave of the son who had come into her life and was now leaving. MaryLou suddenly remembered that hearing was the last sense to go, so they each gave Eric a parting message. Doris said, "You're beautiful, Eric. You were beautiful all the way. You did it just right. You're almost there. I love you!" Eric then died in MaryLou's arms, the peaceful and gentle death he had been promised. The family stood guard in the doorway to prevent the Code Alert and so save the hospital from a routine-induced folly.

Eric, his family, and his doctors all knew he would eventually lose his fight against leukemia. Eric had his family's agreement that when there was nothing more to be done, he should come home to die. What he and his family did not anticipate is that it would be difficult to tell when this moment came and that the final round would catch them in the hospital. Some time during the four-and-a-half years of his illness Eric, his family, and the doctors ought to have had a conference in which they acknowledged that he would eventually need to be moved into the dying role, while leaving open the question of what would determine his entering it. Unlike coma victims, Eric was able to speak and did speak: he asked if he could rest when he was exhausted with battling his illness. In view of the extraordinary tenaciousness and courage with which he lived his life, this should have been taken very seriously, and indeed, MaryLou and his mother had all the clues they needed to determine his readiness to enter the dying role. Their problem was that although death existed for Dr. Dowling, the dying role did not, and he therefore insisted on treating Eric beyond the point where he could gain any benefit. It was not callousness which caused him to behave that way—Eric's mother says that he loved Eric—but rather he saw no options except the one role he knew how to confer, the sick role. Eric's presence in the hospital led Dr. Dowling to imagine that all the decisions were his to make.

The family ought to have been able to say "The time has come for Eric to enter the dying role," and the doctor ought to have known what they were talking about.

Without the concept of the dying role, one is as likely to err in one direction as in the other, and there are known instances in which people have been accorded the dying role when they were not dying. One such instance concerns Dr. Kubler-Ross, well known for her belief that the denial of death on the part of both patients and doctors is at the root of the difficulties people experience in making a good end. In a film presentation shown on the Canadian Broadcasting Company, August 1, 1970, Dr. Kubler-Ross can be seen interviewing patients while her residents look on. One of those interviewed was a rugged truck driver about thirty years of age. He had been told he had Hodgkin's disease and was going to have surgery the next day. When told his diagnosis, he went home and looked it up and learned he had from five to ten years to live. Dr. Kubler-Ross asked him what he felt about death, and he said, deadpan, "I don't know. I've never been dead before." He went on to say that he felt well at present but did not know how he would feel in four years and 364 days. He seemed to be a tough and straightforward person, not given to speculation about the future, and it was evident that Dr. Kubler-Ross was enjoying him and approved of him. In speaking about him she said that of four hundred dying people she had come across very few like the truck driver and that it was remarkable that one as young as he should have accepted his mortality. In other words, she saw him as an exemplary holder of the dying role. The only snag was that he was not in the dying role for the best of reasons: he was not dying. He accepted Dr. Kubler-Ross's probings about his views on death and dying with friendly amusement because he knew he had a fighting chance and that much could happen in the five to ten years that he was likely to live. Far from being an example of someone in the dying role, he was an excellent example of someone accepting the sick role in a serious and potentially dangerous illness. He was going to have surgery the next day, which would be quite unnecessary if he were dying. Just because someone has a form of cancer does not mean that they are dying or that they ought to be in the dying role.

Another instance of this phenomenon concerns a nurse who was taking a course on death and dying based on Dr. Kubler-Ross's work. She visited the cancer ward of a hospital in search of dying people to interview. As she peered into the various rooms on the ward, she found that many of the patients, who were indeed dying, were in no shape to be interviewed. At last she found one woman sitting up in bed looking quite alert. She asked this patient if she would consent to be interviewed. The woman agreed, and the nurse began to inquire, à la Kubler-Ross how she felt about dying. Now the woman was in the hospital for diagnostic tests because she feared that a tumor had recurred, but at that moment she was not even in the sick role, let alone the dying role. After the nurse departed, the woman found herself deeply depressed. She pulled out of her depression only when she realized that the nurse had by implication said that she was dying when in fact she was not. The nurse, with the best of intentions, had inadvertently (though briefly) plunged the woman into the dying role. What this shows is that one can learn a great deal about death and dying without learning anything about the dying role.

All roles can be played well or badly, indifferently or brilliantly. Those who turn in a brilliant or memorable performance illuminate the role for all of us and give us a chance to do it better ourselves, even if we are not great actors. The Huxleys—Aldous, Maria, and Laura—have greatly contributed to our grasp of the dying role. Few of us have their resources, but all may learn from their performance as told by Laura Archera Huxley in *This Timeless Moment*.

In 1955, Maria Huxley came home from the hospital when it was realized that nothing further could be done for her and that she was dying of cancer. An old friend who was a psychotherapist came and put her into a hypnotic state in which she was told she would have no more nausea and it would be possible to keep down liquid nourishment and water: from that point on, no further intravenous feeding was necessary. Her husband Aldous spent many hours of each day sitting with her. He, too, used hypnotic techniques to keep her as physically comfortable as possible. But he addressed himself mostly to the deeper levels of her mind, the levels on which she had known mystical experiences when they lived in the Mojave Desert. The days passed and she grew weaker; Aldous told her to "let go, to forget the body, to leave it lying there like a bundle of old clothes, and to allow herself to be carried, as a child is carried, into the heart of the rosy light of love." Then he told her, "No memories, no regrets, no looking backwards, no apprehensive thoughts about your own or anyone else's future. Only light. Only this pure being, this love, this joy. Above all, this peace. Peace in this timeless moment, peace now, peace *now!*" Then she stopped breathing and died without any struggle.

Eight years later Aldous himself was dying of a fatal cancer. His second wife, Laura, faced the difficult problem that he did not seem to know he was dying, and yet she knew dying was very important to him as an expansion of awareness, rather than as an unconscious slipping away. Surely he wanted to die as he had written of death in his novel *Island*. At first she thought he was demonstrating that organic protectiveness which enables some people to conceal from themselves the fact they are dying. Then she realized it was far more likely that he was simply practicing what he preached: to live here and now whether you are going to die tomorrow or in a hundred years. And so until the very end of his days he was working—now with her help, since he was physically too weak to write—on his essay "Shakespeare and Religion." During the last few days of his life, he learned to use a tape recorder to do his writing, and he quickly realized it was a new and interesting way to write. He said, "Yes, I can see how one could do this. . . . It is different . . . quite different. . . . One has to think the phrase through. . . ." He was still learning, even as he wrote his last six hundred words.

When Aldous realized that the labor of dying might lessen his awareness, he prescribed his own medicine, like the moksha-medicine he had written of in *Island*, L.S.D. He had written to Humphry Osmond, "My own experience with Maria convinced me that the living can do a great deal to make the passage easier for the dying, to raise the most purely physiological act of human experience to the level of consciousness and even spirituality." Aldous now wrote on his tablet, "Try L.S.D. 100 mm intramuscular." Laura gave it to him, and now, acting as his guide, said, "Easy, easy, and you are doing this willingly and consciously and beautifully—going forward and up, light and free, forward and up toward the light, into the light, into complete love." His breathing became slower and slower and then stopped.

The way in which the dying role is occupied depends very much on the personality of the role holder. Charles Lindbergh played the dying role very differently than the Huxleys, and in a manner entirely consistent with the way he lived. In 1972, Lindbergh learned he had a lymphoma. Radiation therapy provided a welcome relief, and he was able to resume his conservation missions, including his trip to visit the gentle Tasaday. In August 1974, according to Milton Howell's article in the *Journal of the American Medical Association*, he called from his hospital room in New York to the village of Hana, in Hawaii, "This is Charles Lindbergh. I have had a conference with my doctors and they advise me that I have only a short time to live. Please find me a cottage or a cabin near the village. I am coming home to Maui." Thus he moved himself unequivocally from the sick role to the dying role.

Having flown the five thousand miles on a stretcher, he had eight days in which to complete the plans for his last flight. His sense of timing was, as always, superb. He supervised the building of his eucalyptus wood coffin and the construction of his grave. He planned what he would wear (a khaki shirt and cotton pants) and asked that those attending his funeral wear work clothes. He planned his funeral service, what would be sung and said. He said goodbye to his family. Then he died.

In *Lindbergh,* his biographer, Leonard Mosley, said of him, "He made a lot of mistakes in his lifetime, but not on the journeys he made into the unknown. No word came of his safe arrival. But those who knew how carefully he prepared all his flights were pretty sure that he made it."

It is not surprising that men and women who have great personal resources are able to make a good death, but it appears that very small children do astonishingly well in the dying role. Dr. Lawrence Singer of Children's Hospital in Minneapolis reports that children of three and four seem to know well enough when they are very ill and recognize the need for treatment. They will submit to this with fortitude and behave courageously. They also seem to know when they have had enough treatment and will say so. In a program, "All Things Considered," broadcasted on July 12, 1977, he described one five-year-old who said he did not want any more treatment because it was not helping. His doctors agreed and he died peacefully. Dr. Singer does not believe in lying to the children because it does not work and loses their trust.

It is very puzzling exactly how these children learn the dying role, since they are unlikely to have seen death in their home and they are too small to have read about it. They do not hear long sermons about death as did their Victorian counterparts. The possibility that dying behavior is innate is at first glance improbable, but, in view of the great antiquity of the dying role, it may require further scrutiny.

Dr. Ida Martinson, of the University of Minnesota School

of Nursing, heads the nation's first home-care program for children dying of cancer. She now estimates that eighty percent of children dying of cancer could die at home if they wished and their parents felt they could handle it. Nurses in this program provide home visits as necessary. So far no doctor has had to make a home visit to these children, although they would willingly do so. According to an article by Harry Nelson which appeared in the *Los Angeles Times*, of the children in the program who have died at home, most have died in the living room, often surrounded by their brothers and sisters.

Another possibility for those who wish to make a good death is the hospice. Terminally ill people come into St. Christopher's Hospice in England when their families can no longer cope and when hospitals are no longer appropriate. The people who come to St. Christopher's are not in the sick role, so there is no need for medical treatment. There is no X-ray, no operating room, no pathology laboratory, no Code Alert. Because the dying role is explicit, everything is done to make life as interesting and enjoyable as possible. Dogs are welcome, a baby elephant once visited, and a nursery for staff children provides a steady supply of small children. One patient told Katherine Whitehorn, who was writing an article for *The Observer*, "Where I was before, they stick you away in the corner with an oxygen cylinder; here there's a bit of life."

St. Christopher's was started by Dr. Cicely Saunders, a nurse who became a doctor in order to better equip herself for providing a good place for people to die. The two chief functions there are to ease pain without turning people into vegetables and to help people who aren't going to recover to come to terms with it. Dr. Saunders says, "Pain's physical, social, mental, and spiritual—you have to work out which is which and treat the right one." As to telling people they are going to die, the staff never lie, but they don't force the information, either. One man, greatly relieved to know that he was dying, told Ms. Whitehorn, "I couldn't think what had gone wrong with my marriage."

Patients who feel well enough to go home are encouraged to do so, with the understanding that they can come back at a moment's notice if things get worse. Each year, a few who go home, confound the doctors, and stay home for good. "Hope," Dr. Saunders said, "there's always hope. Even if you can't hope for a cure, you can hope for a good night, or to see your daughter's wedding, or to enjoy a good meal."

How do doctors fare in making a good end? In the dying role they do about as well or as badly as the rest of us. One doctor we know, who had developed liver cancer, went home to die when it became clear the hospital had done all it could for him. He became steadily weaker but remained conscious and cheerful. One day he told his family he was very tired and wanted to go to sleep. He died quietly within the hour, his family close around him, thus confounding his colleagues who had predicted he would be in a coma for about a week. Knowing him, we are sure that out-foxing his doctors added some gentle fun to his tranquil departure.

Other doctors are not so fortunate. Professor Kerppola installed himself in the dying role without the agreement of the other participants in the drama, thus causing unnecessary suffering for himself, his family, and his medical attendants. We know of another case in which everyone *except* the dying doctor knew he was dying. His wife and son made the decision he was not to be told and his visitors were asked not to discuss this with him. Since he probably suspected he was not likely to live, this enforced silence must have been a great strain on everyone. Those who knew him could not help but discuss among themselves the probability that he was dying, which must have made their visits to him even more false. This doctor died at home but without ever having been inducted into the dying role, and so he was cut off from saying goodbye to his family and friends.

The most likely way to speed the change toward a more realistic and humane approach to death is for those in the sick role to accept the fact that they have a right to the dying role if they need it, and for them and their relatives to insist that they not be deprived of it. The failure to give the dying role is a mistaken custom which now has to be abandoned both for reasons of common sense and common humanity. The tides of life and death cannot be stayed by medical activities, and it does little good to patients, their families, the public, or the medical profession to act as if doctors had the elixir of life. The wonders of modern medicine have postponed death for many but prevented it for no one. We owe God a death.

Afterword

Afterword

WITHIN LIVING MEMORY, most children learned about sickness and death in the perilous but familiar surroundings of their own homes. These encounters, sometimes fatal and always frightening, were usually directed by the family doctor, who was helped by the patient's family and friends. Nursing had to be entrusted to these loving amateurs who were often terrified by their own lack of skill and fearful of contracting the illness they were helping to nurse. Those children who survived such ordeals acquired a deep understanding of the nature of the sick role and everything connected with it. Today, not only is serious illness in the early years of life less frequent, but should there be even a hint that something is amiss, the sick child will be rushed to the hospital.

Now, many patients enter the hospital without any previous experience with serious illness and without having lived in a home where someone was seriously ill or dying. As we have shown, acquiring and maintaining oneself in the sick role can be difficult enough for the seasoned patient. It is even harder for the unseasoned patient to leave his normal role and enter the wholly unfamiliar sick role when suffering the many distresses of his first serious illness.

But it's not only the patient who is affected by a lack of training in the sick role. Increased good health among today's young people has also had a direct impact upon the training of doctors and nurses. Medical and nursing schools naturally choose applicants who are healthy and have a history of good health. This is sensible, for these two professions require only those who can devote themselves wholeheartedly to the treatment and care of the sick—ailing doctors and nurses are a liability for patients. Today's candidates for these two professions must acquire an appropriate feeling for their patients; they have to be much more sympathetic than those who were chosen forty to fifty years ago, yet there is little evidence that those who train doctors and nurses have taken notice of this. Doctors who know little about the sick role, either from personal experience or from formal teaching, are likely to have difficulty in using their Aesculapian authority properly, and their lack of experience with the sick role is likely to make them even worse patients and so more vulnerable than ever before.

What can we do to remedy this insidious danger, derived from fortunate circumstances which we cannot possibly regret and would not alter even if it were possible? At the moment, neither the sick role nor Aesculapian authority have a large place in medical education, nor are they discussed by those who plan and run medical services and institutions. The question is where to start.

We believe patients must, above all else, strive to avoid the loss of role we have called becoming a nithing. Lacking a role, you have no goal; when this happens you do not know what to do and cannot tell what others expect of you.

The role in question may be the sick role, the "psych" role, the guinea-pig role, the impaired role, or the dying role. Whichever it is, you must be able to ask, "Am I in that role, now? Is it the proper one for me? What are its rights and duties? How can I undertake them for the best results?" If one is not in the appropriate role, one must find out which role is, and seek to acquire it without delay.

Throughout history, families and cultures which supported the sick role were more likely to survive than those which did not. We know of no culture in which the sick role does not exist in some form, however rudimentary. For doctors, expertise in the sick role is important not only for the sake of their patients, but also to ensure their personal survival and to maintain their professional esteem.

The Aesculapian authority with which doctors are invested is durable and adhesive, but its exercise is not compatable with the proper filling of the sick role. Doctors who are unable to divest themselves of their authority when ill are liable to pay with their lives. Those who misuse their authority become a danger to their patients, the public, their profession, and themselves. For the safety of all, it must be contained, shielded, and aimed with careful deliberation. Yet so far as we know, there has been very little written about this unique medical attribute.

The rise of the nursing profession has often served to enhance, even exaggerate, the doctor's authority. Nursing authority is not identical with that of the doctor and does not derive from it. Its roots are in the family's duty to care for the sick individual. Some of the control over the use of Aesculapian authority can and should come from the nurses' concern for the good of the patient. This can be especially valuable when doctors become preoccupied with technical values and forget the patient's human needs. Nurses have, in fact, often exerted a kind of moral authority, but lack of an appropriate language for discussing and describing this aspect of nursing has made it difficult to study and has prevented us from understanding the principles involved.

What, then, can we do to improve the quality of treatment and care which we are likely to receive? This is hardly an academic matter because our survival may depend upon our getting the very best from our doctors and nurses. As in the past, there are many suggestions for attaining a goal which we all agree is good. Such is the human condition, that medicine can never be good enough and nursing never devoted enough to calm our fears and sustain our hopes. Since the earliest times, medicine has provoked hope, fear, and suspicion, often of an extravagant kind.

It is curious that medicine is today being subjected to criticism as harsh as any aimed at it during its long history. We are the ungrateful and complaining heirs to over a century of medico-scientific miracles. Yet there are many people alive today who can recall times when there were no antibiotics; when anesthetics were crude; operations which are safe today were chancy; blood transfusions were seldom done; complications were frequent; and recovery was slow, uncertain, and often marred by relapses. Doctors then were as well-esteemed as they are today. In spite of their poor results they were trusted, lawsuits were few, and their prestige was high.

In recent years, attempts have been made to redress what is thought to be an imbalance of power to the patient's disadvantage by means of laws, lawyers, and litigation. This has occurred mostly in the United States and some of those who advocate its use seem to envisage transposing the adversary system, which is a feature of law and lawyers, to medicine. But the structure of the law makes it unsuitable in most situations where urgent action is required. Not everyone considers that the satisfaction of dying with one's civil rights intact is better than surviving without benefit of advocacy. Exposés and legal advocacy are aimed at insuring better behavior by doctors, but they have a disadvantage of lowering *swanelo* and so damage the doctor-patient relationship which cannot accommodate intrusive third or fourth parties.

Many books have been written urging us to concentrate on public-health and preventive medicine rather than waste our time on sickness, the cult of hygeia rather than the cult of panacea. These works make excellent reading for the healthy, but when ill most people find them irritating and depressing. One of us recalls treating and diagnosing a naval coxswain, suffering from syphilis, tuberculosis, and a back injury sustained while drunk. The three conditions are all preventable and should have been prevented. However, to have reproached this man with his failure to avoid syphilis and with incurring his back injury due to drink and then to have accused the navy of letting him get tuberculosis would have been both futile and insulting; worse still, it would have jeopardized the chances of getting his full cooperation and trust for treatment. A censorious attitude, however good it might have been for teaching him a lesson, might have endangered his life. Doctors only reproach patients with established illnesses when their behavior interferes with treatment and imperils recovery. The errant coxswain was an excellent patient.

Preoccupation with science medicine is seldom helpful to any sick person. Some people find scientific conundrums fascinating, however sick they are, but this is not a universal taste and some patients object strongly to being perceived as guinea pigs by their doctors.

As patients, every one of us needs a map of the terrain. That map must concern itself not with illness in general, or even with illness of a particular diagnostic category, but with our own unique, personal illness which we are confronting now. The map must have coordinates, references which can be given to the sick person quickly, clearly, simply, and kindly.

The coordinates for the map consists of a description of the various roles available, the authority of those involved in the medical drama, and their rights and duties. The relationships among various role holders and the diagnosis are also essential references. It is only when all of these matters have been made explicit does it become possible for the patient, doctor, nurses, and family to see where they stand and agree to participate in moving toward an attainable goal.

Any doctor with clinical experience knows the patient's active and willing participation is an essential ingredient for successful treatment. The involved, responsible patient has not only a higher status than those who are irresponsible and uninvolved, but is perceived as being a better person and hence acquires prestige.

Principles are one thing, but putting them into practice is not always simple. It would undoubtedly be better to start learning about these matters before becoming seriously ill. The longer one has enjoyed good health the more prudent it would be to acquire this information before one enters the hospital. It is surely worth taking stock of one's situation and learning how to use our map of the strange country of illness even when the circumstances are far from ideal.

Once ill, we become the greatest expert regarding our own illness. If the illness is a rare one, then doctors and nurses will be greatly helped by patients who can give an exact account of their experience, but even in quite common illnesses, the cooperative, observant patient can help clinicians to acquire greater understanding, and this will be of use and benefit others.

In the last analysis, the kind of service we as users of medicine get depends upon just what we as employers of doctors and the people who build and staff the hospitals demand. We are likely to get the kind of medicine we deserve. Medicine can be hopelessly bureaucratised, fettered by lawyers and the fear of lawyers, the prey of accountants and actuaries, dominated by an arbitrary uncontained Aesculapian authority, or be the plaything of more or less scrupulous politicians. If we are determined and serious enough, a medicine aimed at ensuring that those who treat the sick have the opportunity to do their best and in which the patients are encouraged and helped to fill their role well can be evolved. We have the knowledge to do this, and from time to time, in spite of the many obstacles and hazards described here, the sick role is performed splendidly. But it seems that changes within medicine itself, mostly unrecognized, are endangering this ancient and excellent social invention. We cannot and should not abandon the benefits of modern medical technology and the sciences which have made these possible, but modern medicine will never deliver its full benefits unless those human relationships which nurtured medicine and made its development possible are cherished, enlarged, and strengthened.

It is sometimes suggested that any attempt by the public to improve medicine will never be allowed unless it meets with the complete approval of the medical profession. As we have shown, doctors suffer as much as anyone from these shortcomings of medicine, but at the moment there is no common language between doctors and patients to improve the level of discourse, enlarge understanding, and so increase *swanelo*. It is our belief that we have provided some of the ideas and words for such a language, and it is our hope that others will join us in putting this language to good use.

Because we are mortal, subject to accidents, illness, and the subtle assaults of time, medicine must fail; but that failure need not be absolute. It can and often has been transformed by moving from the sick role to the dying role. When this is done an overwhelming medical defeat undergoes an alchemical transmutation, and sometimes emerges as a triumphant enactment of the dying role.

To succeed in such an extraordinary reversal calls for understanding of both these roles, an ability to move deftly from one to the other, and a refusal to become a nithing. By giving up the struggle to survive, the dying are able to devote their physical, moral, and spiritual resources to the last reaches of life.

When this change of goal occurs with the new role, the

dying person has the right to support from family, friends, and all of us. Medical necessities no longer predominate, and medicine becomes a means of helping to achieve that good end which has replaced recovery as the new goal. The end of life, like its beginning, is mysterious, and in the face of its questions we are all ignorant. Sages and saints, who know more than the rest of us, have shown by example that hope, joy, and inspiration may spring from witnessing a good end. And that this can be renewed in the telling for hundreds and even thousands of years. Our studies show that both old and young people today still die in a manner which inspires those about them.

Some hold a good death is an end in itself: the final curtain, while for others life is a painted veil screening us from a reality which lies beyond. No matter; for those whose last act does crown the play, their dying enriches the survivors helping them to live better and giving them an example of how well to die, when their time comes. Few of us can leave a better legacy.

References and Readings

References and Readings

Aldington, Richard. *D. H. Lawrence*. New York: Collier Books, 1967.

Altman, Lawrence K. "Doctor and Patient: Bill of Rights a Break With Old Paternalism." *The New York Times*, January 10, 1973.

American Hospital Association. "A Patient's Bill of Rights," 1975.

"Amputation Battle." *The New York Times*, January 30, 1977.

Anonymous, M.D. *Confessions of a Gynecologist*. New York: Bantam Books, 1974.

Armstrong, Dale. *Hang In There*. New York: Grossman Publishers, 1974.

Ashkenazy, Irvin. "Judy Has Myasthenia Gravis." *Reader's Digest*, November 1972.

Beaumont, William. *Experiments and Observations on the Gastric Juice and The Physiology of Digestion*. New York: Dover Publications, 1959.

Berkman, Paul. "Survival, and a Modicum of Indulgence in the Sick Role." *Medical Care* 13(1975):90.

Bernard, Claude. *An Introduction to the Study of Experimental Medicine*. Translated by Henry Copley Greene. New York: Dover Publications, 1957.

Berndt, Catherine H. "The Role of Native Doctors in Aboriginal Australia." In *Magic, Faith and Healing*, edited by Ari Kiev. New York: Free Press, 1974.

Blumenthal, David S.; Burke, Robert; and Shapiro, Arthur K. "The Validity of 'Identical Matching Placebos,' " *Archives of General Psychiatry* 31 (August 1974):214–15.

Boswell, James. *The Life of Samuel Johnson*. Abridged and edited by Frank Brady. New York: Signet Classics, 1968.

Bowen, Elenore Smith (Laura Bohannen). *Return to Laughter*. Garden City: Doubleday Anchor, 1964.

Butler, Samuel. *The Way of All Flesh*. New York: Signet Books, New American Library, 1960.

Cardamone, Joseph M. "Notions preconceived a tangled web we weave." *Modern Medicine*, February 15, 1975.

Celsus, *On Medicine*. Translated by W. G. Spencer. *The Loeb Classical Library*. Cambridge: Harvard University Press, 1935.

Cooper, I. S. *The Victim Is Always the Same*. New York: Harper & Row, 1973.

Darling, John P. "The Story of My Epilepsy: The Fortunate Fate of a Stubborn Fool." In *When Doctors Are Patients*. See under Pinner, Max, and Miller, Benjamin, eds.

Davis, Fred. *Passage Through Crisis: Polio Victims and their Families*. Indianapolis: Bobbs-Merrill Company, 1963.

De Beer, Sir Gavin. *Charles Darwin*. Garden City: Doubleday Anchor, 1965.

Dewhurst, Kenneth. *Dr. Thomas Sydenham: 1624–1689*. London: Wellcome Historical Medical Library, 1966.

Eareckson, Joni, and Musser, Joe. *Joni*. Minneapolis: World Wide Publications, 1976.

Federn, Erndst. "How Freudian Are the Freudians?" Originally published by Merck, Sharp, and Dohme, Inc., in *Reflections*. West Point, Pa., 1968. Reprinted from *Journal of the History of the Behaviorial Sciences*, July 1967.

"Florida Hospital Sues to Evict Girl in Coma," *Los Angeles Times*, November 12, 1974.

Fox, Renee. *Experiment Perilous*. New York: Free Press, 1959.

Freud, Sigmund. *The Question of Lay Analysis, with Freud's 1927 Postscript*. Translated by James Strachey. Garden City: Doubleday Anchor, 1964.

Friedman, Marcia. *The Story of Josh*. New York: Ballantine Books, 1974.

Gluckman, Max. "The Reasonable Man in Barotse Law." In *Everyman*

His Way, edited by Alan Dundas. Englewood Cliffs, N.J.: Prentice-Hall, 1968.

Goldsmith, Norman. "Multiple Sclerosis." In *When Doctors Are Patients*. See under Pinner, Max, and Miller, Benjamin, eds.

Gottlieb, Julius. "Viventa Viventibus Intelligunt: An Account of Coronary Artery Disease, Coronary Occlusion and Gall Bladder Colic." In *When Doctors Are Patients*. See under Pinner, Max, and Miller, Benjamin, eds.

Greenburg, Samuel. " 'Say, Doc, I got this pain . . .' " *Life*, Vol. 68, No. 18 (May 15, 1970).

Griffith, Valerie Eaton. *A Stroke in the Family*. Harmondsworth, England: Penguin, 1970.

Grotjahn, Martin. "A Psychoanalyst Passes a Small Stone with Big Troubles." In *When Doctors Are Patients*. See under Pinner, Max, and Miller, Benjamin, eds.

Gunther, John. *Death Be Not Proud*. New York: Pyramid, 1962.

Halberstam, Michael, and Lesher, Stephan. *A Coronary Event*. Philadelphia: J. B. Lippincott, 1976.

Hart, Moss, and Kaufman, George S. *The Man Who Came to Dinner*, 1939.

Howell, Milton M. "The Lone Eagle's Last Flight," *Journal of the American Medical Association*, Vol. 232, No. 7 (May 19, 1975):715.

Hunt, Nigel. *The World of Nigel Hunt*. New York: Garrett Publications, 1967.

Huxley, Laura Archera. *This Timeless Moment*. New York: Ballantine Books, 1968.

Jonas, Doris F. "Life, death, awareness, and concern: a progression." In *Life After Death*, edited by Arnold Toynbee and Arthur Koestler. New York: McGraw-Hill, 1976.

Jones, Ernest. *The Life and Work of Sigmund Freud*. Abridged and edited by Lionel Trilling and Stephen Marcus. Garden City: Doubleday Anchor, 1963.

Kaufman, Barry Neil. *Son-Rise*. New York: Harper & Row, 1976.

Keller, Helen. *The Story of My Life*. New York: Dell, 1972.

Kennedy, B. J. "Pleasures and Tragedies of Death." *Journal of the American Medical Association*, Vol. 234, No. 1 (October 6, 1975):24.

Kerppola-Sirola, Irma. "The Death of an Old Professor." *Journal of the American Medical Association*, Vol. 232, No. 7 (May 19, 1975):728–29.

Kirkup, James. "A Correct Compassion." In *The Scientific Back-*

ground, edited by A. Norma Jeffares and M. Bryn Davies. London: Isaac Pitman & Sons, 1958.

Kopp, Sheldon. *If You Meet the Buddha on the Road, Kill Him!* New York: Bantam Books, 1976.

Kramer, Heinrich, and Sprenger, James. *Malleus Maleficarum.* Translated by Rev. Montague Summers. London: Pushkin Press, 1948.

Kroeber, Theodora. *Ishi in Two Worlds.* Berkeley: University of California Press, 1961.

Kubler-Ross, Elizabeth. "Let's Only Talk About the Present." *The New York Times*, January 15, 1973.

Lamb, Charles (Elia). "The Convalescent," in *Last Essays of Elia* (July 1825). *The Portable Charles Lamb*, edited by John Mason Brown. New York: Viking Press, 1969.

Lame Deer, John, and Erdoes, Richard. *Lame Deer: Seeker of Visions.* New York: Simon and Schuster, 1972.

Lesher, Stephan. "After a Heart Attack." *The New York Times Magazine*, January 27, 1974.

Levit, Rose. *Ellen: A Short Life Long Remembered.* New York: Bantam Books, 1974.

Lewis, Aubrey. *The State of Psychiatry.* New York: Science House, 1967.

Lofting, Hugh. *The Story of Doctor Dolittle.* Philadelphia: J. B. Lippincott, 1920.

Low, Merritt B. "Poliomyelitis with Residual Paralysis." In *When Doctors Are Patients.* See under Pinner, Max, and Miller, Benjamin, eds.

Lund, Doris. *Eric.* Philadelphia: J. B. Lippincott, 1974.

McCance, R. A. *Reflections of a Medical Investigator.* London: Pitman Medical Publishing Co., Ltd., 1959.

Macmichael, William. *The Gold-Headed Cane.* 1826 Facsimile Edition, London Royal College of Physicians, 1968.

Major, Ralph A. "Sir James Paget." In *The Quiet Art*, edited by Robert Coope. London: E. & S. Livingston, 1952.

Massie, Robert K. *Nicholas and Alexandra.* New York: Dell, 1971.

Massie, Robert K., and Massie, Suzanne. *Journey.* New York: Alfred A. Knopf, 1975.

Medawar, Peter D. *Induction and Intuition in Scientific Thought.* London: Metheun & Co., Ltd., 1969.

Meering, Otto von. "Medicine and Psychiatry." In *Anthropology and the Health Sciences*, edited by Otto von Meering and L. Kasdan. Pittsburgh: University of Pittsburgh Press, 1970.

Miller, Floyd. "Dr. Cotzias and I." *Reader's Digest,* September 1975.

Molière. *The Feast of the Statue,* in *Comedies.* Translated by Baker and Miller. London: J. M. Dent and Sons, Ltd., 1961.

Montague, Ashley. *The Elephant Man.* New York: Ballantine Books, 1973.

More, Henry. "Letter to Anne Conway." In *A Peck of Troubles,* edited by Daniel George. London: Jonathan Cape, 1936.

Mosley, Leonard. *Lindbergh.* New York: Dell, 1977.

Nance, John. *The Gentle Tasaday.* New York: Harcourt, Brace, Jovanovich, 1975.

Neal, Patricia. "Patricia Neal: 'Despite Tragedy, Love Gives My Life Meaning,' " *Family Weekly,* February 12, 1978.

Nelson, Harry. "Nontraditional Holistic Methods Little Understood, Seem Kooky." *Los Angeles Times,* December 25, 1977.

———. "Home Care for Children Dying of Cancer Supported," *Los Angeles Times,* April 7, 1977.

Nemy, Enid. "When Severe Illness Plays Havoc With Family Life." *The New York Times,* August 15, 1973.

Nolen, William A. *Surgeon Under the Knife.* New York: Coward McCann & Geoghegan, Inc., 1976.

Osmond, Humphry, and Siegler, Miriam. "Doctors as Patients." *The Practitioner* 218 (June 1977):834–39.

Owen, John. "Epigrams." In *Analecta Psychiatrica,* edited by J. R. Whitwell. London: H. K. Lewis, 1946.

Park, Clara. *You Are Not Alone.* Boston: Atlantic-Little, Brown, 1976.

———. *The Siege.* Boston: Atlantic-Little, Brown, 1972.

Parsons, Talcott. *The Social System.* New York: Free Press, 1951.

Paterson, T. T. "Notes on Aesculapian Authority." Unpublished manuscript, 1957.

Pemberton, John. *Will Pickles of Wensleydale.* London: Geoffrey Bles, 1970.

Pickles, William. *Epidemiology in Country Practice.* Bristol, England: John Wright, 1939.

Pinner, Max, and Miller, Benjamin, eds. *When Doctors Are Patients.* New York: W. W. Norton & Co., Inc. 1952.

"Practice from a Proscrustean Bed." *Medical News,* November 14, 1977.

Prince, Raymond. "Indigenous Yoruba Psychiatry." In *Magic, Faith and Healing,* edited by Ari Kiev. New York: Free Press, 1974.

Quinlan, Joseph, and Quinlan, Julia, with Phyllis Battelle. *Karen Ann: The Quinlans Tell Their Story.* Garden City: Doubleday, 1977.

Ramsey, Paul. *The Patient as Person*. New Haven: Yale University Press, 1970.

Rebeta-Burditt, Joyce. *The Cracker Factory*. New York: Macmillan Publishing Co., Inc., 1977.

Robinson, Donald. "How Well Do Lawyers Serve the Cause of Justice?" *Birmingham News*, August 11, 1974.

Roueché, Berton, ed. *Curiosities of Medicine*. New York: Berkley Medallion Book, 1964.

Sacks, Oliver. *Awakenings*. New York: Vintage Books, 1976.

Samter, Max. "Deafness." In *When Doctors Are Patients*. See under Pinner, Max, and Miller, Benjamin, eds.

Schwartz, A. Herbert. "Children's Concepts of Research Hospitalization." *New England Journal of Medicine* 287 (September 21, 1972):589–92.

"750-Lb. Man Asks for Help." *The Trentonian*, September 26, 1969.

Schary, Dore. *Sunrise at Campobello*, 1957.

Siegler, Miriam, and Osmond, Humphry. *Models of Madness, Models of Medicine*. New York: Macmillan Publishing Co., Inc., 1974.

Singer, Lawrence. "All Things Considered." Alabama Public Broadcasting Station, July 12, 1977.

Solzhenitsyn, Aleksandr. *Cancer Ward*. New York: Bantam Books, 1969.

Stanley, Sir Henry. *Catalogue of an Historical Exhibition*. London: Royal College of Physicians, July 5–October 3, 1973.

Starett, Vincent. *The Private Life of Sherlock Holmes*. New York: Pinnacle Books, 1975.

Stevenson, Ian. "Observations on Illness from the Inside (Bronchiectasis)." In *When Doctors Are Patients*. See under Pinner, Max, and Miller, Benjamin, eds.

Sydenham, Thomas. "The Doctor." In *Doctors by Themselves*, edited by Edward F. Griffith. Springfield: Charles C. Thomas, 1951.

"Teenager dying of cancer is welcomed to Waikiki." *Birmingham News*, February 17, 1975.

Thompson, Jesse E. "Sagittectomy—First Recorded Surgical Procedure in the American Southwest, 1535." *New England Journal of Medicine* 289 (December 27, 1973):1403–1407.

Warner, W. Lloyd. *A Black Civilization*. Gloucester, Mass.: Peter Smith, 1969.

Waugh, Evelyn. *Brideshead Revisited*. Harmondsworth, England: Penguin, 1962.

Welch, Adrienne. "Parents aided in coping with crib death." *Birmingham Post-Herald*, August 29, 1974.

Wertham, Fredric. "A Psychosomatic Study of Myself." In *When Doctors Are Patients*. See under Pinner, Max, and Miller, Benjamin, eds.

West, Jessamyn. *The Woman Said Yes: Encounters with Life and Death*. New York: Harcourt, Brace Jovanovich, 1976.

Whitehorn, Katherine. "No screens around the beds." *The Observer Review*, July 20, 1975.

Wiggers, C. J. "Human Experimentation as Exemplified by the Career of Dr. William Beaumont." In *Clinical Investigations in Medicine: Legal, Ethical and Moral Aspects*, edited by I. Ladimer and R. W. Newman. Boston: Boston University Law-Medicine Research Institute, 1963.

Williams, Barbara. *Albert's Toothache*. New York: E. P. Dutton, 1974.

"Woman Risks Life to Stand Straight." *Midnight*, October 27, 1975.

Woolf, Virginia. "On Being Ill." In *The Moment and Other Essays*. London: The Hogarth Press, Ltd., 1947.

Young, Stephen B., and Countryman, Vern. "Responsibility for a 'Sacred Trust.' " *The New York Times*, May 12, 1974.

Yuncker, Barbara. "Hospitals Mixed on 'Patient's Rights.' " *New York Post*, November 28, 1973.

Zelman, Samuel. "The Case of the Perilous Prune Pit." In *Curiosities of Medicine*, edited by Berton Roueché. New York: Berkley Medallion Books, 1964.